Fundamental Finance

First Edition

Fundamental Finance

The Plain English Financial Education Everyone Should Have

Douglas Denhartog

Format	**ISBN**
eBook	978-1-7358200-1-9
Hardcover	978-1-7358200-2-6
Paperback	978-1-7358200-0-2

For bulk orders, email:
partnership@fundamental.finance

For additional information, visit:
https://www.fundamental.finance/

This book was possible thanks to:

My mom, who I am confident made the right choice

My dad, whose perpetual effort is most admirable

My aunt, and her unconditional love

My uncle, who showed me how to have a voice

My grandma, and her dutiful conviction of purpose

My grandpa, who might as well have been named Stalwart

Relentlessly pursue your wildest dreams
with balance and purpose

Table Of Contents

Preface

Who Fundamental Finance Is For

Fundamental Finance is for anyone interested in learning the essential financial concepts everyone should know. Importantly, you do not need any prior financial knowledge to understand the concepts and explanations we will explore in plain English.

It is a myth that only privileged elites can be wealthy. Finance, money, and investing are intimidating only because you were never taught the fundamental financial concepts everyone should know. This book will provide you with the financial education you never received from your parents, high school teachers, college professors, or favorite Internet influencers.

While writing Fundamental Finance, I regularly asked myself, "will my grandparents understand this?" And after reading the original draft, my beloved grandma with Alzheimer's and dementia thought this "science fiction thriller is simply wonderful." Thus, my hope is you too will think Fundamental Finance is "simply wonderful."

Why Fundamental Finance Exists

Fundamental Finance exists to provide you with the plain English financial education everyone should have. Importantly, Fundamental Finance is not a get-rich-quick

~~scam~~ program where I pretend to have some ~~fake~~ formula that will ~~never~~ make you wealthy. Instead, Fundamental Finance will explain: (i) what money is; (ii) how your money can work for, or against, you; and (iii) a multitude of other important financial concepts everyone should know.

Benjamin Franklin believed "an investment in [education] always pays the best interest." Agreeing in principle, Nelson Mandela said, "education is the most powerful weapon which you can use to change the world." So do yourself a lifelong favor and arm yourself with the financial education you need to make informed financial decisions.

Understanding and applying the information in this book will take work. And yes, there *is* a learning curve. But the reward of having, and applying, a financial education far outweighs the required effort. After completing Fundamental Finance, I am confident you will be armed with Nelson Mandela's most powerful weapon necessary to make more informed financial decisions: a financial education.

What Fundamental Finance Contains

Much of the information covered in Fundamental Finance is available in the world in disorganized chunks, scattered across hundreds of physical books, blog posts, and online videos.

While some of this information can be accessed for free, much requires some kind of purchase. Regardless, there is no shortage of information available. In fact, too much information is part of the problem.

Obtaining a financial education is often overwhelming precisely because there is too much information available. Often poorly organized, if even organized at all. But more often than not, it is just a mountain of disorganized information that might as well be written in Latin.

Fortunately for you, this book concisely demystifies the abundance of unorganized information. Moreover, I know exactly what it is like to be overwhelmed by financial illiteracy. I am not one of those lucky few who received a financial education early in life.

I did not grow up in a wealthy family with parents who taught me everything I needed to know about finance. I have worked long hours, week after week, at boring jobs only to earn minimum wage (which was only $6 an hour).

There were plenty of months during my early twenties where I squeaked by with less than $1 in my bank account in the months I managed to avoid $35 overdraft fees, all while simultaneously owing over $35,000 on a new vehicle I should never have purchased.

My financial ignorance and discomfort convinced me I did not want to barely survive paycheck to paycheck for the rest of my life. And like any good infomercial, I knew there had to be a better way. I decided I wanted to be debt-free and financially literate.

It took me four years to pay off the debt I owed, but I succeeded in becoming debt-free. While paying off my debt, I spent hundreds of hours accumulating as much financial knowledge as I could. After paying off my debt, I began saving and investing.

At first, I felt pretty silly saving $1 here and $5 there. But I stuck with my new lifestyle of saving and investing. Eventually, ones turned into hundreds, hundreds became thousands, and thousands are now hundreds of thousands. But importantly, I started $1 at a time.

Since 2010, I have invested thousands of personal, professional, and academic hours and energy learning and using the financial concepts explored in this book. The hundreds of hours I spent writing this book focused on curating, organizing, and simplifying the most important financial concepts everyone should know.

Resultantly, Fundamental Finance contains concise, carefully crafted information and enables you to avoid spending (because I already have) thousands of hours of your own time over the next decade attempting to figure out everything in this book.

But armed with the financial knowledge in this book and with thousands of hours given back to you over the next decade, I am confident you will be able to make more informed financial decisions compared to having never read Fundamental Finance.

However, Fundamental Finance is not meant to be a comprehensive, 500-page almanac. Many concepts covered in this book are introduced and briefly explained, with just enough detail to kickstart your financial education. With plenty more concepts and detailed explanations being beyond the scope of this book.

Resultantly, some readers might feel Fundamental Finance is, how did Ben Affleck put it in *Good Will Hunting*, "rather elementary." Nevertheless (as my good friend Alec would say), I am confident Fundamental Finance will help cement any reader's understanding of the concepts we will cover while exploring the basic building blocks of financial literacy in plain English for complete beginners.

Depending on when you are reading this book, I may have already published follow-on books to Fundamental Finance, titled Introductory Investing and Intermediate Investing. These follow-on books build upon the concepts covered in this book and provide the plain English investing education everyone should have.

How Fundamental Finance Is Organized

I present the information in Fundamental Finance from both a top-down and bottom-up perspective. Using the human body as an analogy, the top-down approach is equivalent to describing the major parts of the human body:

(i) the brain, muscles, bones, et cetera and (ii) how these major parts come together to form a human body.

The bottom-up approach is equivalent to describing how the brain functions, how muscles contract, or how bones break. In other words, the bottom-up approach explores specific details about specific major parts.

From a top-down perspective, each chapter in Fundamental Finance focuses on one specific, major financial concept. Collectively, these concepts and chapters comprise what I believe are the most essential, foundational financial concepts everyone should know.

From a bottom-up perspective, each chapter contains individual, labeled sections which explore specific details of the chapter's concept. Each section contains just enough detail to emphasize the essential information, while avoiding being so detailed the section should be its own chapter or book.

And most importantly, I promise to use plain English and avoid esoteric financial jargon. So rest assured, every chapter, section, detail, and example will be understandable, straightforward, and in plain English. Further, I **bold** every important concept we define, in the sentence it is defined.

Free Fundamental Finance Supplements

I was completely serious when I said Fundamental Finance exists to provide as many people as possible with the financial education I wish someone had provided me.

My belief that everyone should obtain a financial education is so strong, that rather than not read Fundamental Finance and receive no financial education, I would rather you receive a financial education from somewhere else rather than no financial education at all.

To that end, if you think Fundamental Finance is not appropriate for you, I encourage you to explore the list of supplemental financial education resources I included in the Appendices.

Just keep in mind, even though this list contains what I believe are free, high-quality supplements to Fundamental Finance, I created Fundamental Finance because I believe none of these resources, on their own or combined, provide the concise, plain English financial education you will obtain from Fundamental Finance.

And even if you do complete Fundamental Finance, which I hope for your sake you do, the supplemental resources in the Appendices are still worth completing in addition to the education you will receive from Fundamental Finance.

Either way, I implore you to obtain a financial education. I am incredibly excited to embark on this journey with you and introduce you to the most important financial concepts everyone should know. Let's get started.

Saving And Investing

Introduction

There are significant differences between saving, investing, trading, and speculating. And unfortunately, many people consider investing, trading, and speculating to be: (i) identical and (ii) merely synonyms for gambling.

However, saving, investing, trading, and speculating are very, very different activities. And while we will explore saving, investing, trading, and speculating in more detail throughout this chapter, the following plain English analogies will get us started.

Saving is like putting tree seeds in a box to save for later so you can plant the seeds sometime in the future. **Investing** is akin to planting the tree seeds you saved because you want to grow a tree for any combination of: beauty, shade, and fruit.

Trading is similar to selling your box of saved tree seeds today because you think you will be able to buy a box of seeds less expensively tomorrow from someone else. **Speculating** is like buying or selling an unlabeled box that may or may not contain tree seeds. But hey, you might end up with some tree seeds, or just an empty, useless box. Why not take a chance?! It could be fun! Go big or go home, baby!

Simple enough explanations for starters, right? See! I told you I would use plain English. Fear not. You got this! But let's define two additional words before we continue.

Income is money you *receive* from other people (for example, money you receive from working). While **expenses** are money you *give* to other people (for example, rent you pay your landlord each month). With these six definitions behind us, let's move on and explore: saving.

Saving

Let's build on our original understanding that saving is like putting tree seeds in a box to save for later so you can plant the seeds sometime in the future. **Saving** is the accumulation of the difference between your income and your expenses (assuming, hopefully, your income exceeds your expenses).

Savings Formula

Savings = Income - Expenses

Like saving seeds in a box, saved cash can literally be stored in a box on a shelf in your home. But preferably, a "savings box" is a saving account at a bank. However, as we will discuss at length, saving without *also* investing, is not enough to become wealthy.

Investing (in addition to saving) is necessary because currency in a savings account is not safe from inflation. Cash in a savings account loses purchasing power because of: inflation (which we will cover in detail shortly).

For example, in 2020, $1 is approximately the price of a candy bar. In five, ten, 20 years from 2020, inflation will have caused the exact same candy bar's price to have risen well above $1, to say, $3. Do not believe me? What happened to McDonald's Dollar Menu? Well, it is now called the Value Menu, and nearly every item costs more than $1.

Need more convincing? Ask your grandparents how much it cost for them to see a movie in a movie theater when they were children. According to my grandpa, he paid something close to $0.25 for a movie theater ticket in the 1940s.

Today (2020), a movie theater ticket costs something like $12 to $15. If, in the 1940s, my grandpa put $0.25 into a savings account, he would be unable to withdraw this $0.25 today (in 2020) and purchase a $15 movie theater ticket. Thus, $0.25 has clearly lost the purchasing power to buy a movie theater ticket. Yikes.

Now you might be thinking saving is pointless because of inflation. Absolutely not. Saving is essential because, without any savings, you will not have any money to invest. Saving comes first, then investing. But before we get to investing, we will spend a bit more time on this pesky, invisible enemy of money: inflation.

Inflation

Let's build on our original understanding that inflation is the loss of purchasing power. We will redefine **inflation** as: the permanent increase of the cost of products in an economy. For our purposes, let's define **products** generically, and collectively, a good or service. A **good** is a tangible object (for example, a pair of shoes or a car), while a **service** is a performed task (for example, a car wash or massage).

Inflation; goods; services; products; phew. Let's take a moment and recenter. We are talking about inflation, which is the increased cost of products. For example, let's explore the inflation of a 1-hour massage (a service). A 1-hour massage today might cost $60, but 1 year from now, the exact same 1-hour massage might cost $65. The cost of the massage has *inflated* from $60 to $65.

Because of inflation, we can no longer exchange $60 for a 1-hour massage because the exchange value of $60 has decreased. We must now exchange more money ($65) to get the same exact massage because the exchange value of our money decreased.

Skipping ahead for a brief moment, the three functions of money we will explore in more detail later in this book are: (i) medium of exchange; (ii) measure of value; and (iii) store of value. Today, $60 is measured as $60, and in one year from now, $60 is still measured as $60. However, despite having the same measurement, inflation has caused money's exchange value to decrease.

But because money only has value when exchanged, any money saved (stored) will also have decreased in value. Though, a saver will not feel the effect of a reduction in the value of their saved money until they attempt to exchange their saved money, because $60 in their savings account is still measured as $60.

The opposite of inflation, which is called deflation, can also occur. **Deflation** is the permanent decrease in the cost of products in an economy. Deflation causes the exchange value of money to increase, allowing us to purchase more products for less money. But deflation is the exception, and has historically rarely occurred.

In fact, the 1930s were the only decade in the last 100 years which experienced deflation. Annually, inflation has averaged 3.2% since the 1910s and 3.5% since the 1950s. The table below shows the average and decennial inflation rates in the United States between the 1910s and 2010s:

Average Decennial Inflation Rates

Decade	**Rate (%)**
1910s	10.0
1920s	0.1
1930s	-1.9
1940s	5.6
1950s	2.1
1960s	2.4
1970s	7.1
1980s	5.6
1990s	3.0
2000s	2.6
2010s	1.8
Average since 1910s (%)	**3.2**
Average since 1950s (%)	**3.5**

As you can see in the table above, inflation is always occurring (with the 1930s as the only exception). But why you ask, is inflation happening if inflation is the enemy of money? Good question. While hundreds of factors affect inflation, I will limit our discussion to two concepts: (i) demand-pull and (ii) cost-push.

Demand-Pull

Demand-pull is the concept that as more potential purchasers collectively attempt to buy the same product, other potential purchasers will offer increasingly higher prices to the seller. These competing purchasers enable the seller to sell their product to the purchaser offering the highest price. To further explore demand-pull, let's attend: an auction.

Imagine for a moment you are at an auction to support a local charity. Take a second and think of your favorite dessert. For our example, accept there is only one of this dessert at the auction, and there are 20 other people who also consider this dessert to be their favorite.

When the bidding starts, the other 20 people will bid up the price of this dessert because they are all bidding a higher price than the person before them in an attempt to ultimately win this delicious dessert. The price of the dessert has been *pulled* up to match the *demand* for the dessert, hence the name of the concept: *demand-pull.*

The same pulling up of prices to meet demand happens in ordinary business transactions, and across an entire economy with countless transactions annually, results in demand-pull being a major cause of inflation.

Cost-Push

Cost-push is the concept that sellers will increase the selling price of their products when their business costs increase. Costs can increase because the raw materials for products have been demand-pulled up, or it simply costs more to produce the same product.

For example, eventually, all of the oil near Earth's surface will have been extracted, and oil producers will have to drill farther and farther to find new oil. Resultantly, oil producers will need to spend money on new, deep-drilling equipment required to extract the same product (oil).

These oil producers will then increase the sales price of the oil they sell to pay for the cost of their new, deep-drilling equipment. Thus, the *cost* of the deeper extraction will be *pushed* onto the consumer in the form of a higher sales price, hence the name of the concept: *cost-push.* Having explored demand-pull and cost-push inflation, let's see how money itself can cause inflation.

Money Supply

That is right, money itself can cause inflation because money *itself* can be perceived to be scarce or abundant. When money is scarce, money's value increases. And when money is abundant, money's value decreases. The scarcity or abundance of all the money in an economy is the economy's **money supply**.

One particularly common cause of inflation is when an economy's money supply increases. In the United States, the Federal Reserve has the ability to increase and decrease money supply. To modify money supply, the Federal Reserve can do things like raise or lower interest rates and "print" money.

Generally though, the Federal Reserve does not actually print physical money. So, no, the money printer does not actually go, "Brrrrrrrr!" Instead, the Federal Reserve "prints" money using quantitative easing.

Quantitative easing is when the Federal Reserve, for example: (i) purchases investments (usually bonds) from investors or (ii) lends money to banks. But the Federal Reserve arbitrarily creates new money (out of thin air) it then uses to purchase these bonds and make these loans.

Out of thin air? Yup. The Federal Reserve literally opens up their computer, logs into their bank account, and adds a couple of zeros to their bank account balance. We will not dive deep into how, or why, the Federal Reserve can (and does) quantitatively ease, just know it happens.

We will however cover what happens because of quantitative easing. As a result of quantitative easing, the money supply has increased because the economy now has new, additional money the economy did not have before. And because money supply has increased, money has become more abundant.

Now recall what we briefly stated earlier in this chapter. When money supply increases, the value of money decreases. For example, with more money in the economy, potential purchasers can offer increasingly higher prices for products (which is demand-pull inflation).

By now, you should be able to appreciate just how real of an enemy inflation is to money. And hopefully, our discussion of inflation has made you ask yourself: how can money be protected from inflation? The answer: investing!

Investing

Let's build on our original understanding that investing is like planting the tree seeds you saved because you want to grow a tree for any combination of: beauty, shade, or fruit. **Investing** is when you put your saved money to work for you (assuming, of course, you actually bothered to save).

Investing Formula

Investing = Savings + Risk

Many people think investing is complicated, risky, and only for people who are already wealthy. Permit me to enlighten you: investing is only as complicated and risky as you make it and you will likely never be wealthy unless you invest.

To further illuminate the simple reality of investing, let's discuss two common investing misconceptions, that: (i) investing is merely gambling (risky); and (ii) only people who are *already* wealthy invest.

Why Investing Has The Gambling Reputation

Investing is often mistaken for gambling because gambling is what people are *doing* when they *say* or *think* they are investing. Let's explore this confusion by going grocery shopping. Imagine you tell your best friend you are going to the grocery store. But while you are at the grocery store, you spend your money on lottery tickets instead of groceries.

If your best friend has never been to the grocery store themselves, all your best friend will know is: you tell them you are going grocery shopping, disappear for a while, and always return with no groceries, no money, and useless, losing lottery tickets. Eventually, you and your best friend will think grocery shopping is pretty risky and equivalent to gambling.

Buying an "investment" merely because a friend bought the "investment" is not investing, it is gambling. Buying an "investment" merely because an online influencer or talking head on television recommended the "investment" is not investing, it is gambling. Buying an "investment" you do not understand is not investing, it is gambling.

Many people engage in the above uninformed, risky "investing" behavior. Resultantly, these same people and those around them begin to equate investing with risky gambling. If you want to gamble, go to a casino. If you want to buy groceries, go to the grocery store. If you want to invest, make informed investment decisions, not speculative bets.

But if you *want* to speculate, that is fine too. But call it speculation, not investing. I could go on, but you get the point. This is not to say investing is not risky, because yes, investing has specific risks which can be addressed.

Admittedly, a detailed discussion regarding investment risk management is beyond the scope of this book. But for our purposes, just know avoiding investing because of the fear of risk is not avoiding risk. Because even saving has risk; remember inflation?

So here's the deal, if you choose to not save and invest: you will likely never be wealthy. It is what it is. Which brings us to the second common investing misconception: only people who are *already* wealthy invest.

But Only Wealthy People Invest, Right?

It takes money to make money, right? Wrong! While the wealthy often do invest, wealthy people start investing long before they become wealthy. This is to say, investing is the cause, not an aftereffect, of wealth.

Much like a single seed is ultimately responsible for a full-grown tree, small initial savings and investments are ultimately responsible for wealth. Thinking you need money to make money is like thinking you need a full-grown tree to make a full-grown tree. I truly hope the logical fallacy of this thinking is obvious to you.

Deciding not to invest because you think investing is only for people who are already wealthy is equivalent to not going to the dentist when you have unhealthy teeth because you believe only people who have healthy teeth go to the dentist.

If you never go to the dentist, you likely will not have healthy teeth. But if you go to the dentist, you likely will have healthier teeth than if you did not go to the dentist. Similarly, if you never invest, you likely will never become wealthy. But if you do invest, you have a much better chance of becoming wealthy.

If you think investing is only for already-wealthy people, all you see is the result: wealthy people and healthy teeth. You are ignoring all the time and effort put into achieving the result: the diligent saving and investing and flossing, brushing, and regular dental checkups.

Why Should You Invest

I think we can all agree: (i) healthier teeth are better than unhealthy teeth and (ii) more money in your bank account is better than less money in your bank account. But seeing as how this book is not titled Fundamental Dental Hygiene, let's now explore how investing results in more money in your bank account.

The purpose of investing is to: obtain reward(s) by risking your savings. Investments provide investors with two primary **rewards** (which we will also call **returns**): (i) appreciation and (ii) income. Importantly, these rewards can be obtained simultaneously because investment returns are not mutually exclusive. We will now explore each investment reward, starting with: appreciation.

Appreciation

Appreciation is the increase of the *price* of an investment. The keyword here is price, *not* value. Notice, I did not define appreciation as the increase of the value of an investment. Importantly, price and value are two distinctly different concepts and are often conflated with vexing frequency (much like investing and gambling).

However, a proper discussion comparing and contrasting price and value is beyond the scope of this book. For our purposes, just remember price is the amount of money you: (i) pay to purchase and (ii) receive when you sell. While value is what you get. Succinctly: **price** is what you pay, **value** is what you get.

Now back to appreciation. Appreciation happens when you buy something for less money than you sell it for. For example, imagine you buy a rental property as an investment for $200,000 today and sell the same property for $300,000 in the future. In our example, your investment property has appreciated by $100,000. Simple enough right? Now let's look at the second reward investors seek: income.

Income

Income is the payment of cash to you *by* an investment. To explore, let's return to our example rental property investment. The monthly rent checks you receive from your renter is income, not appreciation.

Recall we just learned appreciation and income can be pursued simultaneously? Well, real estate investing is a prime example. The price of the property itself can increase, resulting in appreciation.

Independently and unrelatedly, you receive monthly rental income which has absolutely nothing per se to do with the price of the property itself. Though you can likely charge a higher rent for a higher priced, or more valuable, rental property.

Other common types of investment income are: stock dividends, bond interest, and option premiums. Though exploring each of these individual investment income is unnecessary for our purposes. Just remember, investors seek rewards called: (i) appreciation and (ii) income.

Conclusion

With the basics of saving and investing under our belt, we will cover in the next chapter why you should start investing today rather than tomorrow or a decade from now. As a bit of a spoiler, you should start investing as early in life as possible because investing early will maximize the time your investments can compound.

Now do not fret if the word compounding is new to you, because much of the next chapter is devoted to exploring compounding in great detail. To begin our discussion of compounding, we will start by exploring a concept called: time value of money.

Time Value Of Money

Introduction

To begin exploring the time value of money, we must first consider whether we would prefer to be given:

(A) $100 today
(B) $100 one year from today

If you are like most people, you chose (A) $100 today. But why do most people choose (A)? Well, the answer involves the enemy of money we just learned about: inflation. Additionally, the answer involves investing because we can invest $100 today to receive appreciation and income so we have more than $100 in the future.

If you recall, inflation erodes the value of money over time and has averaged between 3.2% to 3.5% in recent decades. So, for the rest of the book we will always assume annual inflation is 3%.

Given inflation erodes purchasing power, $100 today is equivalent to $103 in one year from today. Said another way, inflation causes $100 today to, in one year from today, have the purchasing power of only $97.

The mathematical calculation to determine the effect of inflation over only one year is reasonably straightforward. Thankfully, the formulas for calculating the effect of inflation over multiple years are only slightly more complicated. These formulas are known as: (i) present value and (ii) future value. We can use these formulas to determine the impact of both: (i) inflation or (ii) investment appreciation.

Future Value

Future Value Formula

Future value = PV * (1 + APR)^N

Future value equates a known present value with an unknown future value based on an assumed interest rate. For example, the future value formula concludes $100 today will be equivalent to $112.55 after four years of compounded 3% inflation.

Ugh, that pesky undefined "compound" word again. I know, I know. We will get to it, I promise. Now let's walk through this future value formula step-by-step, calculating the effect inflation of 3% per year will have on $100 over four years:

Future Value Components

Abbreviation	Name	Value
PV	Present value	$100
APR	Annual percentage rate	3%
N	Number of years	4

Future Value Step-By-Step

Step	Result
Step 1	PV * (1 + APR)^N
Step 2	$100 * (1 + 0.03)^4
Step 3	$100 * 1.03^4
Step 4	$100 * 1.1255
Total ($)	**112.55**

Let's explore future value using a plain English example involving shoes. Imagine today, a pair of shoes you like and want to buy will cost you $100. If you wait four years from today to buy the shoes, and each of the four years you waited experienced 3% inflation, those same exact shoes will cost you $112.55 four years from today.

Similarly, if you invest $100 today and earn 3% each year for the next four years, your $100 will have appreciated to $112.55! Yay! But if your investment returns equal inflation rates, your purchasing power will merely have been maintained.

However, if you do not invest, or your investment returns are lower than inflation rates, your purchasing power will decline. Alternatively, if your investment returns exceed inflation rates, your purchasing power will have increased.

But wait a minute. Isn't 3% of $100 exactly $3? So should not four years of 3% inflation only be $12? How the heck do we end up with $12.55 and not exactly $12?! Well, we will cover why (hint: compounding) after exploring: present value.

Present Value

Present Value Formula

Present value = FV / (1 + APR)^N

Present value equates a known future value with an unknown present value based on an assumed interest rate. For example, the present value formula concludes $88.85 today will become $100 after four years of compounded 3% inflation. Now let's walk through this present value formula step-by-step:

Present Value Components

Abbreviation	Name	Value
FV	Future value	$100
APR	Annual percentage rate	3%
N	Number of years	4

Present Value Step-By-Step

Step	Result
Step 1	FV / (1 + APR)^N
Step 2	$100 / (1 + 0.03)^4
Step 3	$100 / 1.03^4
Step 4	$100 / 1.1255
Total ($)	**88.85**

Let's examine present value using a plain English example. If you have a goal of having $100 four years from today, you will need to invest $88.85 today and earn 3% annually each of the next four years. Alternatively, if a product costs $88.85 today, the same product will cost $100 in four years with 3% annual inflation.

But calculating the future and present value of $100 over just four years only teaches us so much. To fully appreciate the time value of money, we will now shift our discussion to compounding!

Compounding

Albert Einstein is often attributed a statement along the lines of, "compound interest is the eighth wonder of the world. He who understands interest, earns interest. He who does not understand interest, pays interest."

And Einstein was not exaggerating about the wonders of compounding. Second only to a financial education, compounding is the single most powerful tool an investor can use to their advantage. We will begin our discussion of compounding with two concepts: (i) APR and (ii) APY.

APR, or annual percentage rate, is the *basic* interest rate being charged or earned. While **APY**, or annual percentage yield, is the *actual* (or *compounded*) interest rate being charged or earned. Let's explore the difference between: (i) basic and (ii) actual.

For example, let's pretend you put $1,000 into a savings account with a 1% APR. How much interest do you receive? If you answered, "$10," then you are right, *partially*.

However, the question that needs to be answered for a *complete* answer is: how *frequently* do you receive all, or part of, your $10 of interest? Without an answer to this frequency question, we can only know your APR is 1%, but cannot yet know what your APY is.

If your bank pays you 1% APR only once (at the end of the year), your APY will also be 1%. However, if your bank pays you interest multiple times throughout the year, your APY will be higher than 1% *because of compounding*.

If your bank pays you interest once per year, at the end of the year, you will have $1,010. However, if your bank pays you interest every month, you will end up with $1,010.05 at the end of the year (making your APR 1% and your APY 1.005%).

How do we end up with those extra $0.05, you ask? Compounding! "Whoop-de-doo, a whole five cents," you might be thinking. Patience young grasshopper. We are just getting started. Let's continue.

Alright, here it comes. Get ready. Are you ready? You sitting down? Weirdo. Who reads standing up?! Sit down already! Okay, here it is. We end up with those extra $0.05 because each month, we earn interest on the interest we earned in the previous month(s).

Simple enough conceptually, right? So simple even, the concept of compounding might seem unworth of even being talked about. However, do not let compounding's simplicity deceive you, or lull you, into glossing over the rest of this chapter. I implore you to finish reading this chapter with earnest.

Let's now walk through APR and APY step-by-step:

APR And APY Step-By-Step

Month	Beginning Balance ($)	Interest Earned ($)	Ending Balance ($)
1	1,000.00	0.8333	1,000.83
2	1,000.83	0.8340	1,001.67
3	1,001.67	0.8347	1,002.50
4	1,002.50	0.8354	1,003.34
5	1,003.34	0.8361	1,004.17
6	1,004.17	0.8368	1,005.01
7	1,005.01	0.8375	1,005.85
8	1,005.85	0.8382	1,006.69
9	1,006.69	0.8389	1,007.53
10	1,007.53	0.8396	1,008.36
11	1,008.36	0.8403	1,009.20
12	1,009.20	0.8410	1,010.05

As the table above shows, if your bank pays you interest monthly, you end up with $1,010.05 at the end of the year, making your APR 1% and your APY 1.005%.

Your APY is higher than your APR because your monthly interest earns interest in subsequent months. For example, in Month 1, you earn interest on $1,000. But in Month 2, you earn interest on: (i) not only your original $1,000 but also (ii) the interest you earned in Month 1 (which was $0.83).

Alright, APR is straightforward. No math required. But determining APY requires some calculation. The formula to calculate APY is as follows:

APY Formula

APY = (EA - IA) / IA * 100

Let's walk through this APY formula step-by-step using our $1,000 savings account with a 1% APR compounded monthly:

APY Components

Abbreviation	Name	Value
EA	Ending amount	$1,010.05
IA	Initial amount	$1,000.00

APY Step-By-Step

Step	Result
Step 1	(EA - IA) / IA * 100
Step 2	($1,010.05 - $1,000) / $1,000 * 100
Step 3	$10.05 / $1,000 * 100
Step 4	0.01005 * 100
Total (%)	**1.005**

Okay, hold on. Time value of money? Present and future value? Compounding? APR and APY? I thought I promised you plain English. Yeah, you are right. Let's step back for a moment and just talk about the intellectual concept of compounding.

Compounding is merely the word we use to describe (i) what exists today depends on (ii) what existed yesterday. Let's start with a plain English example: a tree. Remember those tree seeds you saved in that box?

A tree exists physically where it is today because a seed was planted there a long time ago. In addition to being planted, the seed received water and sprouted roots. After sprouting roots, the tree grew a little each day as it absorbed sunlight, water, and nutrients in the soil. So the nice, big, shady tree you see today with juicy, juicy mangos is the result of all the days of compounding (or growing) upon its former self.

In fact, everything is the result of compounding. You name it: cars, airplanes, crops, computers, smartphones. Everything. Everything that exists today is the compounded result of what existed before it; even civilization itself. That is right. Everything. Again, everything is the result of compounding.

Disagree? I, and ~~Mr. Lebowski~~ The Dude, would respond similarly, "yeah, well, you know, that is just like, uh, your opinion, man." Marvel villain Thanos would tell you, "dread it; run from it; [compounding happens] all the same." And Star Wars anti-villain Darth Vader would menacingly warn, "you underestimate the power of [compounding]."

Alright, enough about trees and humanity. We shall return to our discussion about compounding *money*! Most of you are familiar with the adage, "money does not grow on trees." Technically correct, money does not *actually* grow on any tree. But, money *can* compound (or grow) exactly like how a tree compounds.

With money, compounding is the reinvestment of previously earned investment returns, which themselves subsequently earn investment returns. In other words, **financial compounding** is: investment returns earning investment returns. Thus, our investments today are the compounded result of our prior investments.

We introduced the concept of earning money on earned money earlier when we discussed APR and APY. However, this discussion was overly simplistic, not only in duration (12 months) but also in amount ($1,000) and APR (only 1%).

You see, the longer money is allowed to compound, the more money you will have compounding. And the higher your APR, the greater your investment appreciation will be.

To fully explore the power of compounding, I would like to introduce you to: Jackie and Jason.

Jackie and Jason both: (i) are 22 years old; (ii) are recent college graduates with identical degrees and graduation dates; and (iii) earn the exact same amount of income each year working full-time. Further, assume both Jackie and Jason will: (iv) receive 7% APR on their investments; (v) reinvest their investment returns; and (vi) retire when they are 65 years old.

Finally, let's assume: (vii) their 7% APR is paid once annually at the end of the year (which, for those connecting the dots, means their APY is also 7%). **Please note:** these seven assumptions remain constant, unchanged, and true for all four of the compounding scenarios we are about to explore.

Compounding Scenario 1

Jackie (who read this book in college) decides to start investing immediately upon graduating from college. Jackie invests $1,000 every year for ten years, and then, *never* invests another penny *ever* again.

Jason (who did not read this book in college) decides, instead of investing, to spend $1,000 per year on vacations, new clothes, and drinks every Friday night for each of the first ten years after graduating college.

But after ten years, Jason finally reads this book and decides to start investing $1,000 per year, and continues to invest $1,000 per year until turning 65 years old. Let's pause here for a moment and consider which investor you think will have more money at age 65:

(A) Jackie
(B) Jason

But before we cover their investment returns, let's explore their savings. The table below shows Jackie saves $1,000 a year for ten years (age 22 to 31), saving a total of $10,000. While Jason saves $1,000 a year for 34 years (age 32 to 65), saving a total of $34,000.

Compounding Scenario 1: Total Savings

Age	**Year**	**Jackie ($)**	**Jason ($)**
22	1	1,000	0
. . .	. . .	. . .	. . .
31	10	10,000	0
32	11	10,000	1,000
. . .	. . .	. . .	. . .
65	44	10,000	34,000
Total ($)		**10,000**	**34,000**

The table above shows the annual and total savings of both Jackie and Jason. But as we have already learned, investing savings is required to become wealthy. So, let's examine what happens when Jackie and Jason *invest* their savings. **But before we move on, I want to make three critical points extremely clear.**

First, I am not trying to pull a fast one on you. There is no "catch." **Second**, I am not doing something sneaky to make the results end up a certain way. The results are what they are; no gimmicks. And **finally**, what I am about to show you is nothing more than the simple power of financial compounding.

Resultantly, the ***only*** differences between Jackie and Jason are: (i) when they start investing (Jackie at 22 and Jason at 32) and (ii) how many years they save and invest (Jackie for 10 years and Jason for 34 years). Jackie and Jason, and their investment returns, are otherwise identical per our original seven assumptions.

Hopefully you are satisfied everything is as above board, transparent, and legitimate as Dominion Voting Systems. I would never intentionally mislead you. Alright, let's find out who has more money at age 65. Drum roll please!

Compounding Scenario 1: Results

	Total Saved ($)		**Total Invested ($)**	
Age	**Jackie**	**Jason**	**Jackie**	**Jason**
22	1,000	0	1,070	0
. . .	. . .	. . .	. . .	. . .
31	10,000	0	14,783	0
32	10,000	1,000	15,818	1,070
. . .	. . .	. . .	. . .	. . .
65	10,000	34,000	147,512	137,237
Total ($)	**10,000**	**34,000**	**147,512**	**137,237**
		Return ($)	**137,512**	**103,237**
		Return (%)	**1,375**	**304**

As the table above shows, at age 65, Jackie will have $147,512 while Jason will have only $137,237. That is right! Jackie will end up with more money than Jason *because of the power of compounding*. Jackie ends up with more money than Jason despite Jackie saving and investing only $10,000 while Jason saved and invested $34,000.

Amazing really. *My favorite part is*: Jackie enjoyed spending $1,000 each year Jason saved $1,000. Yet at age 65, Jackie still ended up with more money than Jason. So remember this: saving and investing *is* compatible with spending money and enjoying life. In fact, saving and investing results in having *more* money to enjoy spending.

Eventually, in Compounding Scenario 3, we will consider what happens when Jackie continues to save and invest each of the 44 years between age 22 and 65. But first, let's consider the results when Jackie and Jason each save $6,000 per year instead of just $1,000.

Why $6,000 per year? Because $6,000 is the current (2020) contribution limit for an individual retirement account (IRA). We will discuss IRAs in more detail later in this book. But for now, just know an IRA is a special kind of bank account specifically for investors and retirement.

Compounding Scenario 2

For Compounding Scenario 2, assume all the same facts as Compounding Scenario 1. Except now, Jackie and Jason each save and invest $6,000 per year instead of just $1,000. As the table below shows, at age 65, Jackie will have $885,075 while Jason will have $823,421.

Compounding Scenario 2: Results

	Total Saved ($)		Total Invested ($)	
Age	Jackie	Jason	Jackie	Jason
22	6,000	0	6,420	0
. . .	. . .	. . .	. . .	. . .
31	60,000	0	88,702	0
32	60,000	6,000	94,911	6,420
. . .	. . .	. . .	. . .	. . .
65	60,000	204,000	885,075	823,421
Total ($)	**60,000**	**204,000**	**885,075**	**823,421**
		Return ($)	**825,075**	**619,421**
		Return (%)	**1,375**	**304**

Compounding Scenario 3

For Compounding Scenario 3, assume all the same facts as Compounding Scenario 2. Except now, Jackie saves and invests $6,000 *every* year for 44 years (not just the first ten years). As the table below shows, at age 65, Jackie will end up with $1,708,496 while Jason will again end up with only

$823,421. Jason again ends up with $823,421 because his assumptions are identical between Compounding Scenarios 2 and 3.

Compounding Scenario 3: Results

	Total Saved ($)		Total Invested ($)	
Age	Jackie	Jason	Jackie	Jason
22	6,000	0	6,420	0
. . .	. . .	. . .	. . .	. . .
31	60,000	0	88,702	0
32	66,000	6,000	101,331	6,420
. . .	. . .	. . .	. . .	. . .
65	264,000	204,000	1,708,496	823,421
Total ($)	**264,000**	**204,000**	**1,708,496**	**823,421**
		Return ($)	**1,444,496**	**619,421**
		Return (%)	**547**	**304**

Compounding Scenario 4

For some readers, saving and investing $6,000 per year might seem unattainably lofty. With this in mind, let's reconsider Compounding Scenario 3, where Jackie and Jason each save and invest every year once they start saving and investing (Jackie for 44 years and Jason for 34 years).

However, for Compounding Scenario 4, let's assume Jackie and Jason only save and invest $1,378 per year. Why $1,378 you ask? Well, $1,378 is a special number we will revisit and explore later in this book. For now though, let's examine the results of Compounding Scenario 4. As the table below shows, at age 65, Jackie will end up with $392,385 while Jason will end up with $189,112.

Compounding Scenario 4: Results

	Total Saved ($)		Total Invested ($)	
Age	**Jackie**	**Jason**	**Jackie**	**Jason**
22	1,378	0	1,474	0
. . .	. . .	. . .	. . .	. . .
31	13,780	0	20,372	0
32	15,158	1,378	23,272	1,474
. . .	. . .	. . .	. . .	. . .
65	60,632	46,852	392,385	189,112
Total ($)	**60,632**	**46,852**	**392,385**	**189,112**
		Return ($)	**331,753**	**142,260**
		Return (%)	**547**	**304**

Do It Yourself: Compounding Calculator

Hopefully, each of the four compounding scenarios we explored have impressed upon you the undeniable power of compounding. While Jason's investment returns may certainly be satisfactory, Jackie's investment returns are comparatively better.

Again, Jackie and Jason each: (i) saved and invested identical amounts per year and (ii) achieved identical investment returns. Jackie achieved investment returns superior to Jason's for one reason, and one reason alone: compounding.

For those interested in exploring compounding further, use ~~Google~~ your favorite search engine to search for: "compounding calculator." Alternatively, you can use the compounding calculator I built for readers of this book at: **https://www.fundamental.finance/investor-calculator/**

My compounding calculator has capabilities not generally available in the other calculators your favorite search engine will show you. Regardless which compounding calculator you end up using, I think you will benefit from (and enjoy) further exploring compounding on your own with a calculator.

Rule Of 72

Before we finish our discussion on compounding, I want to mention: the Rule of 72. The **Rule of 72** is a quickhand method for approximating: (i) the length of time required to double an amount of money (ii) compounding at a specific interest rate.

Rule Of 72 Formula

Rule of 72 = 72 / Interest rate integer

As the formula above shows, to use the Rule of 72, divide 72 by the interest rate integer. For example, the interest rate integer of 6% is 6. Resultantly, $100 compounding at 6% will double in approximately 12 years (72 / 6).

The Rule of 72 is most accurate with interest rates between 6% and 10%. This means the Rule of 72 is actually not a rule, but more like a guideline, since a rule is *always* true. Thus, the Guideline of 72 was likely invented by Caribbean pirates.

I digress. When working with interest rates outside this 6% to 10% range, just 72 for every 3% away from 8%. For example, use 73 if your interest rate is 11% and 70 if your interest rate is 2%. Got that? Have no fear, I made a table.

~~Rule~~ Guideline Of 72 Examples

Interest Rate (%)	Years To Double	Adjustment	Rule
1	70.0	2	70
2	35.0	2	70
3	23.7	1	71
4	17.8	1	71
5	14.2	1	71
6	12.0	0	72
7	10.3	0	72
8	9.0	0	72
9	8.0	0	72
10	7.2	0	72
11	6.6	-1	73
12	6.1	-1	73
13	5.6	-1	73
14	5.3	-2	74

Conclusion

It is quite alarming how few people save and invest. According to a survey by GOBankingRates, "nearly 70% of Americans have less than $1,000 of savings." This should come as no surprise given the Economic Policy Institute found, "nearly half of families have no retirement account savings at all."

Based on the multitude of financial discussions I have had over the years, many people do not save and invest because they think they are too uneducated, too young, or too broke to start saving or investing. Nonsense.

Uneducated? Not after finishing this book. *Too young?* Be like Jackie, and begin compounding your investments as soon as possible. *Too broke?* Unlikely. Nearly everyone has disposable income they spend on: coffee, cigarettes, alcohol, lottery tickets, movie tickets, slurpees, et cetera; I could go on, but you get the point.

We will discuss at length later in this book how saving and investing is a lifestyle. As we will learn, the lifestyle of saving and investing requires a conscious, habitual choice of: paying yourself first. We will also explore a simple, easily achievable habit of: saving only $1 more per week than the week before.

Armed with this simple $1 habit, you will save $1,378 in a single year. If you recall, $1,378 was the amount Jackie and Jason saved and invested in Compounding Scenario 4. Again, more on $1,378 to come when we discuss this $1 habit.

Sadly, saving $1,378 *for just a single year* will result in you having more savings than 70% of all Americans ($1,378 is greater than $1,000). And should you save and invest $1,378 each year for 44 years you could end up with a juicy $392,385 like Jackie in Compounding Scenario 4.

You now have a choice. Armed with the knowledge of the power of compounding, you can choose to either: (i) begin compounding your money immediately like Jackie or (ii) procrastinate like Jason and miss out on the benefits of compounding. But remember, you and you alone are responsible for your choices in life. So, as infamous rapper 6ix9ine put it, "are you dumb, stupid, or dumb? Huh?!"

What Money Is

Introduction

So far, we have spent most of our time discussing: saving and investing (shout out to inflation too though). And even though you might think we have been talking about saving and investing money, we have not been.

Confused? Good. You are right where you need to be. I have intentionally been keeping you in the dark. However, this chapter will be the light in the darkness. But if we have not been talking about saving and investing *money*, what *have* we been talking about saving and investing?! Moreover, what *is* money then, if not the thing we save and invest?

Take a moment right now to think about your definition of what "money" is. The vast majority of people I have asked over the years to define money have come up with a definition similar to: money is (i) the thing I use to pay for the products I buy or (ii) the thing my employer pays me for my work.

For our purposes, we can simplify these common answers into: money is the thing paid by, or to, me for products (which, if you remember, products are goods and services). And for that matter, "paid by, or to" can be simplified into "exchanged," leaving us with: **money** is the thing exchanged for products.

But if you ask an economist to define money, you will likely receive a more academic answer along the lines of money is a: (i) medium of exchange; (ii) measure of value; and (iii) store of value.

The origin of this academic definition of money is often traced back to *Money and the Mechanism of Exchange* (1875), in which William Jevons analyzed money in terms of four functions which were memorialized in the couplet:

Money's a matter of functions four
a Medium, a Measure, a Standard, a Store

However, modern economists generally dismiss the "standard of value" function, which leaves: (i) medium of exchange; (ii) measure of value; and (iii) store of value.

Before we discuss these three remaining academic functions of money, we will first explore the three basic types of money which have existed throughout time. It makes sense to discuss historical money types first so we can refer back to these types of money when we discuss money's functions.

Types Of Money

Three major types of money have existed since societies started using money. The first type of money used was *commodity money*, commodity money was replaced by *representative money*, and representative money has been replaced by *fiat money*. Fiat money is (in 2020) the type of money modern societies currently use.

Each type of money has comparative benefits and drawbacks. And each subsequent type of money attempted to solve the drawbacks of the previous type(s) of money being replaced. With this short background out of the way, we are now ready to explore each of the three major types of money in more detail. We will progress from oldest to newest, starting with commodity money.

Barter Economy

Okay, you caught me. Bartering is not money, and even if bartering was money, it is not commodity money. But let's take a brief moment to discuss what life was like even before any money, much less commodity money.

Before money, people **bartered** by exchanging their products for someone else's products. Imagine this scenario 5,000 years ago: you were a baker and I was a painter. As a baker, all you have is your baked foods (your goods) on full display atop your fancy cake stand (shoutout to my dear friend Sachit) and your ability to bake (your service).

As a painter, all I have is my paintings (my goods) and my ability to paint (my service). Now imagine you wanted one of my paintings. What can you exchange with me for one of my paintings? Hopefully, your answer is baked goods or baking services. Remember, money does not yet exist in our barter economy.

But what if I do not need or want baked goods or baking services? Well, I am not giving you one of my paintings. As you can tell, we are at an impasse because we do not coincidentally want what both of us have to exchange.

This exchange impasse is known as the **coincidence of wants** problem. Coincidence of wants will reappear throughout this chapter, and we will discuss further then. Now though, we will explore: commodity money.

Commodity Money

Commodity money was the first type of money ever used. **Commodity money** was physical, tangible objects, for example: stones, precious metals (for example, gold or silver), seashells, or anything ancient societies thought possessed or represented value.

Commodity money was created to resolve the coincidence of wants problem that plagued barter economies. To explore, let's extend our painter-baker example from before. Now though, a few generations have passed and our society has agreed seashells (a commodity) will be our money. Now, if you (or anyone else) wants a painting, I will accept seashells in exchange for my painting(s). Similarly, you will accept seashells in exchange for your baked goods.

But the practicality of commodity money starts to fade when buying something expensive (for example, a house). How many buckets of seashells would you have to give to the seller of the house? And would you physically deliver every single one of those buckets anyway?

Imagine having to exchange 100,000 seashells in exchange for a house before trucks and forklifts existed. Imagine the incredible number of roundtrips required with a horse-drawn wagon after how many countless hours of manually loading how many buckets of seashells? My muscles are getting sore just writing about it.

So, despite addressing the coincidence of wants problem, early commodity money suffered from an excessive volume problem. Eventually, societies universally adopted precious metals as their commodity money (namely, gold and silver). These precious metals were so highly valued, an amount small enough to carry in your pocket was sufficient to purchase a house.

The second significant problem with commodity money is commodities are inherently limited in supply. There are only so many seashells on the beach and only so much gold in the hillside. But, it is this inherent scarcity that today's commodity money advocates believe gives commodity money value.

However, precious metals are heavy, and nobody is trying to get a workout from walking around with pockets full of heavy, precious commodity money. So society came up with a solution: representative money.

Representative Money

Representative money consists of paper bills or other physical records reliably exchangeable for a fixed quantity of a specific commodity. The value of representative money matches the value of the commodity it *represents*, while not itself *being* the physical commodity it represents.

For example, recall the house and seashell scenario presented when discussing commodity money. Now imagine the buyer deposits their 100,000 seashells into a bank. In return, the bank gives the buyer a piece of paper, which: (i) confirms there are 100,000 seashells deposited at the bank and (ii) enables anyone possessing this piece of paper to withdraw these 100,000 seashells.

This piece of paper is representative money because this piece of paper *represents* 100,000 seashells. Thus, instead of transporting around truckloads of seashells, the buyer can carry around a piece of paper representing truckloads of seashells.

When the United States was on the "gold standard," money was representative of physical gold held by the United States government. Despite representative money solving the considerable problem of having to transport and exchange large volumes of physical commodities, representative money still had numerous problems of its own.

First, like commodity money, the commodity itself can be lost, stolen, destroyed, or devalued. For example, the bank could catch on fire and the seashells could be burned to ash. So, after the fire, if anyone attempted to exchange their piece of paper for 100,000 seashells, the bank would be unable to give that person 100,000 seashells.

Second, the coincidence of wants problem still exists because representative money merely represents commodities and those commodities have to be desired by the people transacting. Though, over time this coincidence of wants problem extinguished because (as we previously mentioned) the commodities used for money became almost exclusively precious metals.

However, the final problem of representative money was representative money's inflexible measure of value. For example, a piece of paper representing 100,000 seashells cannot be torn in half and each half resultantly represent 50,000 seashells apiece.

As we have already discussed, despite representative money eliminating the volume of exchange problem, representative money was not perfect. In pursuit of perfection (lol), societies created fiat money to: (i) eliminate the coincidence of wants problem and (ii) be a flexible measure of value.

Fiat Money

Fiat money is money whose value is not derived from any intrinsic value because fiat money is not itself, nor represents, a commodity. Instead, **fiat money** has value only because a society agrees their fiat money has value.

For example, examine the dollar bills in your wallet. These are pieces of paper with printed designs. You cannot eat dollar bills, nor you cannot plant them. They are just pieces of paper. But you, me, your hairstylist, my grandma, and the mailman all agree $5 is $5.

In a sense, fiat money does not even really exist. Fiat money is just a figment of our imagination. Fiat money only has value because we all agree it does. Moreover, most fiat money today does not even exist in a physical paper or coin form. Most fiat money today exists only as digital records in a computer that change when money is transferred from one account to another.

For example, such a transfer occurs when you use your credit card or send money to a friend using Venmo. Thus, fiat money has become extremely easy to exchange in large volumes (for example, swipe or tap) and is universally accepted (thus, no coincidence of wants problem).

But, fiat money has a severe flaw we have already introduced earlier: inflation (which we will discuss again later in this chapter). Again, because of inflation, fiat money cannot be stored (saved) without losing value. Which again, is why saving without investing is not a fool-proof, risk-free strategy to become wealthy.

Functions Of Money

Having introduced the historical types of money, we can now discuss the functions of money. Our discussion of money's functions will be a high-level overview, but will provide sufficient detail to fully explain the essential points you should be aware of.

Just appreciate some people devote their entire career to studying money's functions. Recall from earlier in this chapter, the three functions of money introduced were: (i) medium of exchange; (ii) measure of value; and (iii) store of value.

Medium Of Exchange

Recall the definition any random person likely gave you when you asked them to define money: "the thing exchanged for products." Unfortunately, this definition of money is, in fact, not a definition of money.

Instead, this definition describes money's function as a medium of exchange. Let's dwell on this mixup for just a moment. Why do people commonly conflate the definition of money with the definition of a function of money?

Well, we humans are simple creatures. How does the saying go? The whole world looks like a nail to a person with a hammer. Similarly, most people (incorrectly) define money based on their primary (or only) relationship with money (as the thing exchanged for products).

Let's revisit the example of exchanging seashells for a house. Without modern money, we would need to exchange hundreds or thousands of buckets of seashells for the house. With modern money, the seashells and house stay put, and we exchange money instead.

Much simpler, right? Thus, money functioning as a medium of exchange solves the coincidence of wants problem. We no longer need two people who coincidentally want to exchange a house for seashells.

In closing, money functions as a **medium of exchange** because money is the medium (thing exchanged, for example, paper bills or digital numbers) exchanged for products. Simple enough to understand. But how do people know how much money should be exchanged?

Measure Of Value

The second function of money is as a measure of value. The value of money is measured in "defined monetary units" created, maintained, and retired by each country's national government. "Defined monetary unit" is a bit academic, so let's stick with a term most people have heard before, "denomination."

For example, in 2020, the United States Dollar is denominated in the following mediums: (i) coins and (ii) bills. Coin denominations (measured in *cents*) are: $0.01, $0.05, $0.10, and $0.25. Bill denominations (measured in *dollars*) are: $1, $5, $10, $20, $50, and $100.

When a new denomination is created, it is "put into circulation." When an existing denomination is taken out of circulation, it is "discontinued." For example, the $10,000 bill denomination from the late 1800s has been discontinued and is no longer usable (but as a collectible is worth far more than $10,000 in 2020, often selling for more than $125,000).

And sometimes, even though a denomination has not been officially discontinued, the denomination is phased out of circulation. For example, the $2 bill which was first issued in 1862. But today, you would be hard-pressed to find anyone who actually had a $2 bill or had even seen a $2 in many years (or ever, shout out to you Generation Z).

Denominations have three distinct requirements: (i) each unit must be divisible into smaller units without any loss of value; (ii) units of the same value must be perceived to be of equal value; and (iii) each unit of measure must be identifiable.

Let's examine the first denomination requirement: each unit must be divisible into smaller units without any loss. Imagine for a moment a $5 bill. This $5 bill can be split into fifths with five $1 bills, or twentieths using twenty $0.25 quarters, et cetera. But five $1 bills and twenty $0.25 quarters still each independently total $5.

Now let's examine the second denomination requirement: units of the same value must be perceived to be of equal value. Imagine you want to include a $20 bill in a birthday card for a friend. Unfortunately, the only $20 bill you have is wrinkled.

However, you want to give your friend a brand-new, unwrinkled $20 bill. So you go to your bank, stand in line, get called by the next available teller, and you explain to the teller that you want to exchange your wrinkled $20 bill for an unwrinkled $20 bill.

If a wrinkled $20 bill were considered to be worth less than an unwrinkled $20 bill, your bank teller would request two things: that you (i) give them your wrinkled $20 bill and (ii) pay a fee to make up the difference between the lower value of your wrinkled bill and the full value of the unwrinkled bill you want.

Imagine! A fee, depending on how wrinkled your $20 bill was?! Who gets to determine how wrinkled your bill is, anyway? See the problem? Some subjective person gets to make an arbitrary decision about the value of your wrinkled

$20 bill. Thankfully, a $20 bill is valued at $20, wrinkled or not. And your bank teller will readily exchange your wrinkled $20 bill for your unwrinkled $20.

Finally, let's examine the third denomination requirement: each unit of measure must be identifiable. Imagine for a moment every United States bill ($1, $5, $10, $20, and $100) were all just blank pieces of paper that were identical in every way (shape, size, and weight). I do not know about you, but all my bills are $100s!

This identifiability is especially crucial for money made of precious metals like gold and silver (which, if you recall, are commodity money), because people may try to keep a little of the precious metal for themselves. To illustrate the point, find yourself a quarter ($0.25) and look at and feel the edge.

Notice the bumpy valleys and ridges? These valleys and ridges are called a "reeded edge." Reeded edges were created to thwart people from stealing some of the precious metal off the coin. Take a step back for a moment and imagine a 100% gold, $50 coin with smooth edges.

What is to stop someone from shaving off a super small amount of gold from this $50 gold coin? Nothing! What if someone was able to shave such a small amount that an average human was unable to tell any gold had been shaved off. Our shaving thief would soon accumulate a lot of gold for themselves and be transacting with gold coins worth only $49.99 that other people thought were worth $50.

With smooth edges, the only way you would know if the $50 gold coin you were receiving had not been shaved is to weigh every gold coin! Ain't nobody got time for that! Thankfully, reeded edges solve this problem because if someone shaves part of a coin, it is readily apparent the coin has been modified. After all, only the shaved portion will be smooth amongst an otherwise reeded edge.

Today, criminals no longer shave off tiny pieces of gold coins, but instead create entirely fake money! Fake money is known as "counterfeit." Governments spend billions of dollars annually trying to thwart counterfeiters by modifying the official design of their money.

With each modification, governments attempt to make counterfeiting more difficult and expensive. And like any crime, governments also impose criminal penalties for counterfeiting (for example, imprisonment and fines).

Store Of Value

The third and final function of money is as a store of value. Money must be able to be reliably saved, stored, and retrieved. Further, the measured value of stored money must remain constant throughout time. For example, if you put $100 in the bank, you need to be able to go back to the bank at any time in the future and be able to withdraw $100.

Fiat money's stored value does not change because fiat money is made of paper, coins, and digital numbers. These mediums do not degrade. Comparatively, imagine if money was made of cheese. Your cheese money will eventually rot and become worthless, having lost all of its value. Thus, you cannot store cheese forever like you can fiat money.

Hopefully, you are still with me despite my having *still* not given you a definition of money. We are getting close, though, as we will finally define money in the very next section. However, we first need to distinguish between money and currency.

The Difference Between Money And Currency

Distinguishing between money and currency is of utmost importance because, almost universally, people are told, and believe, money and currency are synonyms. However, money and currency are two very, very different things. To begin exploring the difference, I must first acknowledge most everything you have read so far in this chapter is not precisely correct.

You see, fiat money is *not* money despite me previously telling you fiat money is a type of money. Fiat "money" is not money, it is fiat *currency*. And even though I previously told you money has three functions, money actually has zero functions. Only currency has functions. But thankfully, the three functions we discussed *are* the three functions of currency.

To quickly recenter, fiat currency: (i) is *not* money and (ii) functions as a medium of exchange, measure of value, and store of value. Unfortunately, fiat currency is a terrible store of value. Remember our discussion about inflation and how my grandpa could buy a movie ticket for $0.25 in the 1940s, but today a movie ticket costs something like $15?

Imagine you saved $0.25 in 1940 (but only saved, and did not invest to earn appreciation/income). Sure, $0.25 in 1940 is still measured as $0.25 in 2020, but $0.25 in 2020 certainly will not buy you a movie ticket. Same currency, same denomination, same measure of value, but terrible store of value.

What Money Is

Former President of Uruguay, José Mujica, touched on the idea of what money is by noting, "when you buy something, you are not paying money for it. You are paying with the hours of life you had to spend earning that money[. Interestingly enough,] life is the one thing money cannot buy."

Former President Mujica understands money is not the currency we use to buy things, and instead, money is an extension of people themselves. Extending the link between time and money mentioned by Former President Mujica, we can begin to understand money is the: (i) manifestation of (ii) accumulated intellectual capital.

Let's explore the individual parts of this initial definition to better understand what money is. **Accumulated intellectual capital** is: all the knowledge and expertise possessed by a person. And if you remember, everything is compounded, even knowledge.

That is right, everything you know today is the accumulated total of everything you knew yesterday plus everything you learned today. Just remember, knowledge is accumulated (compounded) over time.

Manifestation means: acted upon. Suppose you learn something, but never *share* that knowledge with anyone, this knowledge is only accumulated intellectual capital, but *unshared* this knowledge is unmanifested.

Sharing (or manifesting) can occur through *communication* (for example, a conversation between you and a friend over a cup of coffee, or between an author and reader). Sharing can also occur through *action* (for example, you perform a service based on knowledge and skills you compounded).

To summarise, **money** is: (i) knowledge (ii) that has been shared with society. And there is no limit to how much you can learn and share. Meaning there is no limit to the amount of money you can acquire. Let's explore how knowledge can be accumulated and shared by discussing a hypothetical farmer and his son.

Close your eyes for a moment and imagine a modest, 100-acre family farm with rolling hills, chickens, a few cows, and acres of crops. On this farm lives a small family: two parents and a son, named Wayne. Every morning at 5:00 am, Wayne dutifully wakes up before school and helps his father: milk the cows, collect the chicken's eggs, and care for the planted crops.

Day by day, week by week, Wayne learns and repeats these responsibilities. After a year, each of these tasks becomes second nature to Wayne. Now, Wayne can stop here, never learning anything more about farming, yet still successfully help his father run the family farm.

But Wayne has read this book and is particularly interested in farming. So, after school, Wayne spends his free time reading every farming-related: (i) book in his local, public library and (ii) website and blog Wayne can find online. On the weekends, Wayne goes to multiple farmer's markets and talks about farming with the other local farmers.

After weeks, months, and years of learning, Wayne has *accumulated* a significant amount of farming *knowledge*. All this knowledge is accumulated intellectual capital (money) Wayne *can* manifest for currency. I say *can* because, remember, Wayne can accumulate all this knowledge but never manifest it (either because by choice or laziness).

One way Wayne can manifest his accumulated knowledge is by being a more efficient farmer himself. Resultantly, Wayne will receive more currency when he sells his crop because of his increased efficiency.

The Benefit Of Wayne's Accumulated Knowledge

Characteristic	**Father's Knowledge**	**Accumulated Knowledge**	**Benefit (Per Harvest)**
Time to harvest	72 days	60 days	12 days
Cost (per bushel)	$3.00	$2.75	$0.25
Yield (per acre)	180	200	20
Quality rating	90%	95%	5%

The table above juxtaposes crop harvest results using: (i) Wayne's additional accumulated knowledge and (i) just his father's knowledge. For the uninitiated, a "bushel" quantifies a standard amount of crop. For example, a bushel of corn weighs approximately 56 pounds (25.4 kilograms) and (in

2020) sells for approximately $3.50 per bushel. Having explained bushels of corn, we will henceforth presume Wayne is a corn farmer.

Armed with a price per bushel, let's work through some numbers. Using only the knowledge of Wayne's father, the total cost per acre would be $540 (180 bushels * $3.00 per bushel). While the total revenue for 180 bushels is $630 (180 bushels * $3.50 per bushel).

And we will just assume the standard quality rating for a typical bushel of corn is 90%. Thus, the sales price Wayne's dad receives is not adjusted for inferior or superior quality. Resultantly, the dad's knowledge alone results in income of $0.50 per bushel ($3.50 - $3.00), or $90 per acre ($630 - $540).

Manifesting his accumulated knowledge, Wayne achieves a bushel yield of 200 bushels per acre. And at a reduced cost of $2.75 per bushel, the total cost to grow these 200 bushels is $550 (200 bushels * $2.75 per bushel). Lastly, Wayne's total revenue for 200 bushels is $700 (200 bushels * $3.50 per bushel).

However, Wayne's quality is 5% better than his father's, so Wayne receives a 5% increase in sales price. This brings Wayne's total revenue to $735 ($700 * 105%). Under this scenario, Wayne's income is $0.93 per bushel ($3.68 - $2.75), or $185 per acre ($735 - $550).

But wait, there is more! Remember how Wayne's dad was able to harvest every 72 days and Wayne every 60 days? Well, with 365 days in a year, Wayne's father can plant and harvest five times per year while Wayne can plant and harvest six times per year. Meaning, on the 100-acre family farm, Wayne's dad can earn an annual income of $45,000 ($90 income per acre * 100 acres * 5 harvests per year).

However, using Wayne's accumulated knowledge, the family farm can earn annual income of $111,000 ($185 income per acre * 100 acres * 6 harvests per year). Wayne's manifestation of his accumulated knowledge enables the family farm to earn additional annual income of $57,000 ($111,000 - $45,000).

Amazingly enough, we aren't done. You see, so far, Wayne has only shared his accumulated knowledge with his father on their family farm. However, Wayne can also share his accumulated knowledge with his local community. Certainly other farmers would be interested in paying Wayne to teach them how to grow better-quality, higher-yield crop in less time.

For example, Wayne could set up a booth at his local farmer's market and teach other local farmers how to use his advanced and innovative technique(s). Surely other farmers will be interested in learning Wayne's innovative techniques so they too can earn more income for themselves.

But let's scale Wayne's sharing of knowledge because Wayne can share his accumulated knowledge with many more people beyond his local community. For example, Wayne can write a book or create a video course and sell his knowledge to people *worldwide*.

Conclusion

If you manage to remember only one thing from this chapter, remember the following; humans use **currency** to: (i) measure the value of, and as a medium of exchange for, (iii) money (manifested knowledge). For some, the distinction between money and currency might seem esoteric and purely semantic.

Hopefully for you though, the distinction is meaningful and will be instrumental in you obtaining wealth beyond your wildest imagination. However subtle the distinction, understanding the difference(s) between money and currency can be the key to unlocking unimaginable wealth.

"Yeah, yeah, whatever dude. No one cares about the difference between money and currency," you might be thinking, "I only care about how to get more of *it*, what it is!" Well, good news! We will discuss how money and currency are created and obtained in the next chapter as we explore the relationships people have with money.

You And Money

Introduction

If you think small, you will achieve small. If you think big, you will achieve big. If you think poor, you will likely live in poverty. If you think wealthy and live wealthy, you will more likely achieve wealth. Ancient Chinese philosopher, Laozi, explained:

Watch your thoughts, they become your words
Watch your words, they become your actions
Watch your actions, they become your habits
Watch your habits, they become your character
Watch your character, it becomes your destiny

Laozi's truism provides the blueprint for achieving anything in life. Everything starts with your thoughts. Engage life with negative energy, and you will notice and experience negativity. Approach life with positive energy, and you will notice and experience positivity.

Now I am not saying bad things will not happen to good people. Life happens. But getting back up after being knocked down is what matters. How does the saying go, "success is getting knocked down nine times but getting up ten times."

Laozi's truism applies to every aspect of life, from: relationships, to health, and even finances. Thus, if you think, learn, and talk about being wealthy, you will likely take action to pursue wealth. Frequently repeat these wealthy actions, and you will eventually create wealthy habits.

Repeat these wealthy habits, and soon enough, wealth will surround you. For those who *think* I am wrong and *think* it is impossible for you to be wealthy, you may benefit from rereading, and *thinking* deeply about, Laozi's truism.

How Money Is Obtained

Remember, money is accumulated knowledge. Read constantly. Explore constantly. Practice constantly. Fail constantly. Persist constantly. Apply constantly. Learn constantly. Share constantly. Enjoy constantly.

It is 2020, and the Internet has been around for multiple decades. Use the Internet, but not to endlessly scroll social media. Instead, use the Internet to acquire knowledge. By far, the vast majority of my accumulation and manifestation of knowledge has involved a computer.

How Currency Is Obtained

The two primary ways you can acquire currency are: (i) manifesting your accumulated knowledge (working) or (ii) enabling other people to manifest their knowledge (investing). Let's consider both, starting with: manifesting your accumulated knowledge.

Manifesting Your Knowledge

Manifesting your own knowledge is the most common way people acquire currency. For example, most people manifest their knowledge by being an employee who creates or sells their employer's products. When you work for your currency, you exchange your time, energy, and knowledge for currency.

Unfortunately, despite being how most people acquire currency, exchanging time and energy for currency is an incredibly inefficient way of acquiring currency because you have a finite amount of time and energy each day.

Thus, if you work for your currency, the amount of currency you can earn per day is limited by your time and energy. If you only work eight hours a day, you only get paid for eight hours of work.

Typical ways people acquire currency include: hourly wages (for example, as a waitress or cashier); per task (for example, as a gardener or ride-share driver); salary (for example, as a store manager or "white-collar" employee); and self-employment (for example, opening a local coffee shop).

When you work for your currency, currency is an obstacle because you have to work more to get more, because again, you only have limited amounts of time and energy each day. Moreover, when you work for your currency, the amount of currency you receive for your work depends on the value society places on your work.

This is why people are paid more for jobs that require significant knowledge or expertise than for jobs "anyone can do." The perception is people who obtain a bachelor's degree have more knowledge than people who only graduate from high school. This perception is why college graduates often earn more than high school graduates.

Similarly, people who obtain graduate degrees are perceived to have accumulated more knowledge than people who only obtained a bachelor's degree. Most anyone can wait tables and operate a cash register. But not everyone can successfully perform open-heart surgery or write software algorithms to process petabytes of data across a cluster of cloud computing instances.

So, if you want to be wealthy, start by accumulating as much knowledge as you can. Then, share your knowledge with society. And with continually compounding knowledge, opportunities to earn more currency will practically throw themselves at you. But you must also appreciate, you can accumulate all the knowledge you want, but if society does not value the knowledge you chose to accumulate, you will receive little, if any, currency.

For example, you could become the world's most knowledgeable and skilled underwater basket weaver. But if society does not need or want baskets woven underwater, do not be surprised or upset when society does not compensate your knowledge with currency.

If you are looking to acquire more currency, focus on acquiring and manifesting knowledge society is desperate to receive. It will take you the same amount of time to obtain a four-year degree in underwater basket weaving as it will take you to obtain a four-year degree in science, technology, engineering, or math.

Now I am no mathematics savant, but by my calculations, any of the above four-year degrees can be completed in, you guessed it, four years. And though far from omniscient, I am confident underwater basket weavers will earn much less than scientists, technologists, engineers, and mathematicians.

My point is, you choose what knowledge you accumulate and manifest. Thus, you implicitly choose how much currency society will exchange for your accumulated knowledge. Want more currency? Accumulate and manifest knowledge society desperately needs and wants.

In closing, the vast majority of people acquire currency by exchanging their time and energy. However, no matter how skilled you are, the maximum currency you can earn is limited by the number of hours you work per day. For example, top attorneys can charge $2,000 per hour.

But top attorneys are humans just like you and me, with limited amounts of time and energy per day. We all only have 24 hours in a day. And a reasonable assumption is most people only have the energy to work four to 12 hours per day; though a "full-time" workday is eight hours.

Thus, if everyone works roughly the same number of hours per day, the only way to acquire more currency is to increase the value of the knowledge you exchange. This is why, for example, attorneys earn more than cashiers. Because an attorney's legal knowledge is more valuable than knowing how to process a customer order.

Enabling Other People To Manifest Their Knowledge

Enabling other people to manifest their knowledge is just a long-winded way of saying "investing." People who invest their currency have moved beyond working for their currency. They have put their currency to work for them. Suddenly, currency becomes a tool instead of an obstacle, and currency itself creates more currency.

As inefficient as currency might be because of inflation, currency is an extremely efficient worker. Currency does not sleep. Currency does not run out of energy and get tired. Currency can work 24 hours a day, seven days a week, 52 weeks a year, year after year, decade upon decade.

But remember, currency in a savings account is not working for you. Currency in a savings account earns next to nothing. Or worse yet, loses value because of inflation. So again, you must invest your currency if you want your currency to work for you.

But what exactly do I mean by "investing" or "enabling other people to manifest their knowledge?" Well, your employer has enabled you to manifest your knowledge by creating a business and hiring you as an employee. Meaning your employer invested their currency into their business and now uses *your* time and energy to earn income for *them* to spend or reinvest.

Notice how you are the one working, yet your employer is the one earning the income? Well, that is because your employer accumulated enough knowledge to open a business while you merely accumulated enough knowledge to work as an employee in your employer's business.

This employer-employee relationship is amoral, not immoral. This work-income dynamic is merely the result of what knowledge you and your employer *chose* to accumulate and manifest. Remember, everything is the result of compounding. So, if you want to become an employer, start accumulating knowledge to operate a business.

Thus, you can choose to spend your time acquiring knowledge to open your own business, or researching and purchasing investments. For example, you can start a new business based on your accumulated knowledge, purchase rental property, or buy stocks or bonds. And if you make the choice to open a business or purchase investments, you will have put your currency to work for you.

How Wealth Is Obtained

We must first define "wealth" before we can discuss how wealth is obtained. But before we can define and explore wealth, we must first distinguish between being wealthy and being rich. And we will start with what it means to be: rich.

Being **rich** means: having a high income. What is income, you ask? Well, **income** is when you earn currency. And if you recall from earlier in this chapter, you can earn income (obtain currency) when you: (i) work or (ii) invest.

So, the top attorney from earlier who earns $2,000 per hour is likely "rich" by any standard (and certainly *compared* to a cashier who earns minimum wage of $12 per hour). But being rich is not the same as being wealthy. You see, **wealth** means: owning investments.

And, yes, it is possible to be: (i) rich but not wealthy; (ii) wealthy but not rich; (iii) both rich and wealthy; and (iv) neither rich nor wealthy. Let's discuss each possibility by exploring variable life choices by our top attorney.

First, let's explore how someone can be rich but not wealthy. We have already established our top attorney is rich because they earn $2,000 per hour. And we know being wealthy means owning investments. So, despite being rich, our top attorney will never be wealthy if they never save and invest.

Second, let's consider being wealthy but not rich. This can happen when someone has substantial investments (wealth) but low or no income. For example, they have no, or a low paying, job or their investments do not earn income. If you remember from the first chapter, people invest for two rewards: income and appreciation.

Third, let's dissect being rich and wealthy. In this scenario, someone has both: high income and substantial investments. This person may work for their income or have income-paying investments.

But regardless of the source of their income, they also have substantial investments. To have substantial investments, this person may have been rich previously and invested their currency, inherited their wealth, or may have never been rich but over time has purchased many investments.

Finally, let's agree to avoid being neither rich nor wealthy. This means we will: (i) continually increase our income by accumulating and manifesting knowledge society values highly and (ii) saving and investing to increase our wealth. Just remember, income determines richness while investments determine wealth.

How Wealth Is Maintained

Wealth Formula

Wealth = Saving + Investing

If obtaining and maintaining wealth were easy, everyone would be wealthy! Thankfully, the process to obtain and maintain wealth is not a secret, is straightforward, and consists of only four steps:

Wealth Formula Step-By-Step

Step	Description
1	Save by earning more than you spend
2	Invest your savings
3	Maximize rewards and minimizes losses
4	Repeat from Step 1

Simple enough to digest initially. The process of building and maintaining wealth is part art, part science. Let's dissect the science and art of wealth in plain English by using a food preparation analogy.

It is generally accepted cooking is an art and baking is a science. When baking brownies, for example, you: open the packaged box, pour the powdered mix into a bowl, add one egg, the exact amount of water and vegetable oil listed on the back of the box, and mix all the ingredients together.

Then, pour the mixture into a 9x13 dish, place the dish into your 375-degree preheated oven for 11 to 13 minutes, and presto, perfect brownies every time! Pre-packaged, zero thought, and near-guaranteed results. *Science.*

Similarly, the science of wealth is simple: obey the wealth formula and step-by-step above. Obey the formula and four steps, and like baking, you can reasonably expect wealth as a result.

Comparatively, cooking is much less scientific than baking. Add a pinch of this, a dollop of that, season to taste, and saute until golden brown. Oh, and add a garnish and colorful drizzle to round it out.

"Okay, *gulp* I will try my best not to mess *this* up," you think. Sure there is a recipe, but so many steps are left up to your judgment that the recipe is more guidelines than rules.

What is golden brown anyway?! Lots of flexibility, customization, and judgment. *Art.*

Unfortunately, you cannot look at your maybe golden brown saute, recheck the recipe, and confirm you are golden. Recipes do not describe things like golden brown. Similarly, like the missing art not found in recipes, the art of wealth is mysteriously not written anywhere in the wealth formula or step-by-step.

The wealth formula and Steps 1, 2, and 4 are straightforward: save, invest, and repeat. Thus, the art of wealth is Step 3. Step 3 confounds, perplexes, frustrates, and de-wealths most people. And like mastering any learned art (for example, your golf swing or that golden brown saute), mastering the art of wealth takes time, repetition, and hard work.

Again, if obtaining and maintaining wealth was easy, everyone would be wealthy. But if you use this lack of ease as an excuse, then you will likely never be wealthy because you will have given up before you ever began. And if this is what you are thinking, you should reread Laozi's truism at the beginning of this chapter.

Investing Is A Lifestyle

Further, being wealthy (investing) is a lifestyle. Investing is not something you wake up one day and do that day and only that day, and then wake up the next day and avoid. The wealthy consistently save and invest.

In an ideal world, when an investor's income increases, so does their investments. But all too often, increased income goes toward: buying a few more meals out, an unnecessary upgrade of your smartphone merely because your two-year renewal is up again, or perhaps some new monthly membership all your friends are subscribed to.

You deserve to buy those things after all, right? I mean, you worked hard (or invested) and earned yourself more income, right? Right?! I suppose there is some truth to this opinion of right, but at what opportunity cost do these "earned" purchases come at?

Standard Of Living

Standard of living is the quality of life to which you are accustomed. **Quality of life** is what you are used to: the food you are used to eating, the house or apartment you are used to living in, the car you are used to driving, the neighborhood you are used to living in, the $4 latte you are used to drinking, et cetera.

Everyone has their own standard of living. Some people have a more expensive, or "higher" standard of living, while others have a less expensive, or "lower" standard of living. However, people inevitably, and repeatedly, are conditioned to believe their current standard of living is the absolute minimum they can possibly survive on.

Said another way, this conditioning means: former luxuries become new "necessities." Someone who goes on vacation every year expects to go on vacation every year. Someone who always buys a new car will not be happy buying a used car.

No one wants to have had a high standard of living and then be forced into a lower standard of living. Everyone prefers rags to riches over riches to rags. But lowering your standard of living may be necessary to have income to save and invest. But two particularly common obstacles make it very difficult to reduce one's standard of living: (i) lifestyle creep and (ii) golden handcuffs.

Lifestyle Creep

Lifestyle creep is the gradual, incremental increase in your standard of living. Hopefully, after many years of working, you will be earning significantly more income than you did when you first started working. If each year, along with your increase in income, you increase your standard of living, you have succumbed to the trap of lifestyle creep.

And oh, what a nasty trap lifestyle creep can be too. You do not even notice it is happening until it is too late. How can you? Most people are unaware buying that new skirt with your bonus or raise conditions your subconscious to expect you to buy something new every time your income increases.

New skirts turn into upgraded smartphones. Upgraded smartphones become fancier cars. And fancier cars transform into bigger homes. Thankfully, avoiding lifestyle creep is straightforward. All you have to do to avoid lifestyle creep is: not increase your standard of living when your income increases.

Some form of lifestyle creep is unavoidable. Just do not get carried away. For example, as a college student you may not have owed a car. You used the city bus to get to and from your part-time, minimum-wage job during college. You worked hard, graduated, and accepted a full-time, salaried job. Congratulations!

Strict avoidance of lifestyle creep would be to continue using the city bus to get to and from your salaried job. But this might not be possible, or perhaps you decide you want your standard of living to include owning a car. Getting a car is your choice, but after you have driven a car long enough, you will be extremely annoyed if you ever lose the ability to have a car and are forced to revert to using the city bus again.

It is valuable to have: a safe neighborhood to live in, dependable transportation, and experiences with the people you love. But you can have all these yet still spend less than you earn (resulting in savings to invest). You do not need to buy a 3-story, 5-bedroom, 4,200 square foot mansion when a 1-story, 3-bedroom, 2,300 square foot home will do.

You do not need to buy an exotic $100,000 sports car upgraded with the performance package when a $30,000 4-door sedan will suffice. You do not need a $500 designer purse when a $100 store brand is just as stylish.

But you deserve that mansion of a house, exotic sports car, and designer purse! You worked hard and earned enough currency to buy those things! True, you probably did work hard and earn enough currency to buy those things. And you deserve to have the relationship with currency you demand.

If you want to always be working for your currency, go ahead and spend all your currency on these expensive purchases. If you want your currency to work for you, great, buy the smaller home, less expensive commuter car, affordable purse, and invest your saved currency.

Golden Handcuffs

As if lifestyle creep was already enough of a problem, golden handcuffs can be even worse. **Golden handcuffs** are when you are stuck in a situation because of the obligations or benefits you have. Golden handcuffs are often used to describe an employee who is unhappy with their job but finds it difficult to change jobs because of the benefits of their current job.

Maybe their job is close to home, and the commute is short. Maybe their job provides excellent insurance coverage. Perhaps their job allows them to work remotely or has an unlimited vacation policy. Regardless their reasoning, despite being unhappy with their job, they feel unable to leave their current job because of their job's benefits.

For our purposes, golden handcuffs describe the situation where you have a job you do not exactly enjoy, *and* worse yet, you have used debt to purchase a bunch of products (lifestyle creep).

As a result, you cannot leave your job because you have to make required monthly payments to pay for all the products you bought. If you quit your job, all your belongings will be taken from you by your lender because you stopped making your required monthly payments.

The easiest way to put yourself into golden handcuffs is to go into debt to pay for lifestyle creep. Avoiding golden handcuffs then for our purposes means: avoiding needing a high income to pay for an expensive, indebted lifestyle.

Conclusion

I am not suggesting you should be a robot. There is no point in being so frugal you prevent yourself from enjoying life. Everyone wants to enjoy life. But if you start young and follow the simple step-by-step wealth formula from earlier in this chapter, there is no reason why you cannot retire early and drive yourself to fancy dinners in a luxury vehicle!

You just have to decide what you want more: (i) driving a luxury car and eating out every day in your 20s or (ii) retiring twenty years before your peers because you drove an inexpensive sedan, brought lunch from home, and saved and invested what you never spent on a luxury car.

The magic of investing is you will be driving the luxury vehicle and dining in fancy restaurants without having to work like your peers. I will leave you with a quote from LOOK Magazine in 1957 by actor Walter Slezak, and encourage you to avoid "[spending currency] you do not have for things you do not need to impress people you do not like."

Armed with the knowledge of the power of compounding (and the scenarios we explored earlier in this book) would you prefer to be: Jackie or Jason?

Earned Income Taxes

Introduction

Ah yes, taxes. Everyone's favorite financial concept. There are all kinds of taxes, including local, state, and federal: sales tax, income tax, investment tax, property tax, death tax, and more. You name it, your government likely taxes it.

Throughout this (and the next) chapter, we will refer to "**tax authorities**" generically as any federal, state, or local government agency who controls taxation. For example, the Internal Revenue Service (IRS) is the federal government's tax authority, while the Franchise Tax Board (FTB) is California's tax authority.

There are two typical, opposing perspectives people have when it comes to taxes. Some people like taxes, think taxes should be higher, and feel more things should be taxed. While others dislike taxes, think taxes should be lower, and think fewer things should be taxed.

The History Of Taxes

Regardless your perspective regarding taxes, United States tax law has become extremely complex. For our purposes, tax law includes: legislation, statues, regulations, guidance, caselaw, and more. United States tax laws in the early 1900s were only (yes, only) several hundred pages and stayed approximately that size until World War II (1940s).

Tax law changes during World War II increased the page count to more than 8,000 pages. But that was only the beginning. By the mid-1980s, tax law more than tripled, exceeding 25,000 pages. And nearly tripled yet again by the mid-2010s, approaching 75,000 pages.

Seventy-five *thousand* pages of tax rules. What?! Let that sink in. Also, the instructions for a personal tax return was just one page in 1913, but are nearly 200 pages today (2020). Two hundred pages *of instructions*! What the actual duck. Describing United States tax law as "extremely complex" is clearly an understatement.

But how exactly did we get here? Why do we even pay taxes in the first place? Well, taxes have been around for a long, long time. Former Justice of the United States Supreme Court, Oliver Holmes, once said, "taxes are what we pay for a civilized society." Which is to say, taxes exist to fund societal endeavors.

For example, taxes pay for the development of public infrastructure. Public infrastructure includes, for example: roads, highways, sewers, et cetera. Additionally, taxes pay for society's military, police, and fire departments. Further, societies often increase existing, and create new, taxes to fund wars and expansion efforts.

And lastly, taxes are sometimes used to pay the expenses of people with minuscule incomes (known as **welfare**). With an introductory taxation background covered, let's now explore two taxes nearly everyone owes: (i) consumption and (ii) income.

Consumption Tax

A **consumption tax** is added to the cost of a product when purchased by a consumer. Hopefully you recall "product" encompasses both goods and services. But note, few services are affected by consumption taxes, meaning goods are usually the only product affected by consumption taxes. Nevertheless, during our exploration of consumption taxation we will use the term "product" to keep our discussion simple.

Everyone owes the same consumption tax no matter who you are or how rich, poor, or wealthy you are. Anyone purchasing the same product owes the same consumption tax for that product. If you purchase more products (consume more), you pay more consumption tax.

In America, consumption tax is called **sales tax**. There is no federal sales tax in the United States. Instead, each state charges their own, or no, sales tax. For example, a product selling for $100 costs $100 in a state with *no* sales tax (for example, Oregon). But in a state *with* sales tax the same $100 product costs $100 *plus* sales tax (for example, California).

For example, the current (2020) California state sales tax rate is 7.25%. This means any consumer who buys a product in California costing $100 will end up paying *at least* $107.25. And I say "at least," because in addition to state sales tax, each county and city can charge a local sales tax in addition to their state's sales tax.

For example, Los Angeles County charges an additional 2.25% sales tax (meaning the same $100 product costs $109.50 if purchased in Los Angeles County). And some cities within Los Angeles County charge up to an additional 1% (for example, Santa Fe Springs), meaning the same $100 product ends up costing $110.50 if purchased in Santa Fe Springs.

In much of Europe and Canada, consumption tax exists in a slightly different form compared to United States Sales tax. Consumption tax in Europe and Canada is called a **value-added tax** (VAT) and is applied to the "value" added to the product (value added = sales price - cost to produce).

For example, imagine a product costs $60 to produce and sells for $100. VATs would tax the difference between

$100 and $60. A typical VAT rate is something around 17.5%, resulting in VAT of $7 ($40 * 17.5%). In VAT countries, our $100 product is listed on the shelf for $107 and is $107 at the cash register.

Which is unlike America, where the product's list price on the shelf is $100 and sales tax is mysteriously added at the cash register (which my German friend, Florian, is utterly perplexed by). So although the result of both a sales tax and VAT is a more expensive product, the process is slightly different.

Comparing Sales Tax And VAT

Component	**Sales Tax ($)**	**VAT ($)**
Cost to produce	60	60
Value-added	40	40
VAT	0	7
List price	100	107
Sales tax	7	0
Total ($)	**107**	**107**

As the table above shows, the consumption tax (sales versus VAT) occurs at different times, despite an identical end result: a total sales price of $107. In summary, a consumption tax is based on product's sales price. Let's now compare consumption tax to earned income tax, which as we will see in the next section, is imposed on, you guessed it: earned income.

Earned Income Tax

While anyone who purchases products owes consumption tax, only people who earn income owe income tax. Thus, **income tax** is tax owed for earned income earned. But, with more than 75,000 pages of tax rules (and bloating), income tax is, of course, very nuanced. Thankfully, the fundamental concepts are straightforward enough for us to discuss in plain English.

Just remember the following discussion is a general discussion of income taxation and not specific tax advice or instructions. Additionally, our discussion will focus on personal income tax, not payroll taxes like the Federal Insurance Contributions Act Tax (FICA) or Medicare.

Tax Return

Nearly every person who earns any income is legally obligated to file a tax return. Governments punish citizens who earn income but do not file a tax return. So if filing a tax return is a legal obligation, what *is* a tax return? A **tax return** is a collection of required government forms and documentation detailing the: (i) income you earned and (ii) income tax you owe.

Filing a tax return simply means sending your completed forms, documentation, and payment for tax owed to the government. The specific forms and documentation changes over time based on tax law changes. Note, anyone who files a tax return is a **taxpayer**.

United States taxpayers usually need to file two different tax returns, one with each of the: (i) federal government and (ii) state where they earn income. Federal tax returns must be filed by April 15th of the year after the income is earned. For example, tax returns for income earned in 2020 are due by April 15, 2021. And generally, state tax returns must also be filed by the April 15 federal deadline.

Filing Status

Every taxpayer must choose one filing status per tax return. The filing status you choose determines your: (i) standard deduction and (ii) eligibility for certain reductions and credits; all of which will be covered later in this chapter.

Filing statuses can be broadly categorized by marital status (either, married or unmarried).

The two filing statuses married taxpayers can choose between are: (i) married, filing jointly and (ii) married, filing separately. *Filing jointly* means both spouses file a single, combined tax return. Whereas *filing separately* means both spouses file their own, separate tax return. While for unmarried taxpayers, there are three possible filing statuses: (i) single; (ii) head of household; and (iii) widow(er).

The default filing status for unmarried taxpayers is *single*. An otherwise single taxpayer can choose *head of household* if they: (i) owned, paid for at least half of, and lived in a home and (ii) supported at least one dependent who also lived in the home for at least half the year.

A **dependent** is anyone who depends on you for financial support (for example, your children or elderly parents). *Widow(er)* is a filing status virtually identical to *married, filing jointly* which is available: (i) for two years after a spouse's death (I am sorry for your loss) and (ii) if you support a dependent child.

If a taxpayer is eligible to select more than one filing status, most taxpayers choose the filing status which results in the lowest tax owed (more on this selection later). With filing statuses covered, let's dive into calculating tax owed. Calculating your income tax owed can be simplified to:

Simplified Tax Owed Formula

Tax owed = TI * B - C

Simplified Tax Owed Components

Abbreviation	Name
TI	Taxable income
B	Brackets
C	Credits

Okay, okay, if taxes were straightforward and simplifiable, we would not need this chapter. Let alone 75,000 pages of tax rules. Thankfully, when I become President of the United States of America, I will demand a vastly simpler, shorter, more equitable tax law.

Just kidding. But seriously. Okay. Moving on. Let's now examine each component of our simplified tax owed formula, starting with: taxable income.

Taxable Income

Taxable Income Formula

Taxable income = Gross income - Reductions

As the formula above shows, **taxable income** is gross income minus reductions. Simple enough. But what then are: (i) gross income and (ii) reductions?! I am glad you asked.

Gross Income

Gross Income Formula

Gross income = Any income you earn from any source

Wait, **gross income** is *any* income from *any* source? Yes. *Any* income. From *any* source. Period. Get paid for mowing the lawn? Gross income. Have a salaried office job? Gross income. Receive income (for example, dividends or interest) from investments? Gross income. Any income, from any source. Got it? Good. Now let's look at: reductions.

Reductions

Reductions Formula

Reductions = Exclusions + Deductions + Exemptions

We can see from the formula above **reductions** are the sum: (i) exclusions; (ii) deductions; and (iii) exemptions. We will cover each in order, starting with: exclusions.

Exclusions

Exclusions are income(s) which are excluded from taxable income. Most exclusions exist to incentivize specific taxpayer behavior. For example, common exclusions include employer: (i) contributions to retirement investment accounts or (ii) payment of health insurance premiums.

These example exclusions incentivize saving for retirement and providing health care, respectively. Let's explore. Imagine you earn $55,000 by working for your employer. Additionally, let's imagine your employer pays an insurance company $3,000 to provide you health insurance.

And finally, your employer contributes $5,000 on your behalf to a retirement investment account. Given the above assumptions about your employment, how much gross income did you earn?

(A) $55,000
(B) $58,000
(C) $60,000
(D) $63,000

You answered correctly if you decided your gross income was (D) $63,000. Option (D) is correct because the $3,000 in health insurance premiums and $5,000 in retirement account contributions are just as much gross income as is your salary of $55,000.

Remember, gross income is any income from any source. Think of it this way, your employer paid you $63,000. However, your employer decided to pay you: (i) a salary of $55,000; (ii) health insurance worth $3,000; and (iii) $5,000 of retirement funds.

However, the government wants to incentivize employers to provide, and employees to use, company-based health insurance and retirement plans. So instead of owing tax based on gross income of $63,000 you only owe tax based on gross income of $55,000 thanks to exclusions (because employer payments of health insurance and retirement plans are exclusions).

Other common exclusions to gross income include: academic scholarships, gifts, and contributions to retirement investment accounts. Imagine having to pay income tax for every birthday gift you receive or meal someone else buys you. No thank you.

To recenter, exclusions are one type of reduction, and reductions reduce gross income (and thus taxable income). Let's now take a look at another reduction: deductions.

Deductions

Deductions are analogous to ordering a burger at your favorite burger restaurant. You can choose to: (i) build your own burger or (ii) order a pre-made burger already on the menu. Building your own tax burger is called: itemized deductions. Ordering a pre-made tax burger is called: standard deduction.

Unlike an actual burger where you simply order whatever burger you are in the mood to eat, most taxpayers pick the biggest tax deduction burger. But why?

Well, the bigger the deduction, the lower your taxable income. The lower your taxable income, the lower tax you will owe. And just like you would not (should not?) order two real burgers, a taxpayer can use only one of: (i) the standard deduction or (ii) itemized deductions.

Again, a taxpayer must choose either to use the standard deduction *or* itemized deductions, but not both. Generally, a taxpayer only chooses to itemize their deductions if all itemizations, in aggregate, are more than the standard deduction. Do not fret if this last sentence was confusing, all will be revealed shortly.

Suppose a taxpayer's itemized deductions are lower than the standard deduction, and the taxpayer chooses to itemize their deductions. Their taxable income will be higher than if they used the standard deduction, and a higher taxable income usually means more tax will be owed.

The **standard deduction** is a fixed dollar amount nearly every taxpayer is eligible to use to reduce their taxable income. The fixed dollar amount: (i) changes over time based on tax law changes and (ii) depends on the taxpayer's filing status.

Federal Standard Deduction Per Filing Status

Filing Status	**2015 ($)**	**2020 ($)**
Single	6,300	12,400
Married, filing separately	6,300	12,400
Married, filing jointly	12,600	24,800
Head of household	9,250	18,650

The table above shows the federal standard deductions per filing status in 2015 and 2020. As you can see, tax law changes between 2015 and 2020 resulted in dramatically different federal standard deductions per filing status.

To complete our explanation of standard deductions, let's pick up where we left off with our exclusions: with an annual salary of $55,000. Assuming your filing status is single, you would reduce your gross income by $12,400 in 2020 by choosing to use the standard deduction, resulting in taxable income of $42,600 ($55,000 - $12,400).

But why would you choose to, or not to, use the standard deduction? Well, again, that depends on how many itemized deductions you can claim. Unlike the standard deduction, which is a fixed dollar amount any taxpayer is eligible to use, **itemized deductions** are specific expenses a taxpayer can choose to use (instead of the standard deduction) to reduce their gross income.

Common itemizable deductions include: charitable contributions, medical expenses, homeownership expenses (for example, mortgage interest and property taxes), and state and local taxes.

Unless you are a particularly peculiar person, you want to pay as little tax as possible. Thus, choosing between the standard deduction or itemizing your deductions should be straightforward: choose the deduction type which results in the lowest taxable income. Which is to say, pick the largest of the standard or itemized deductions.

Let's explore itemized deductions by again assuming you earn an annual salary of $55,000. To better understand the difference between the standard deduction and itemized deductions, let's consider two scenarios.

The first scenario will explore (i) insignificant itemizable deductions while the second scenario will examine (ii) significant itemizable deductions. Let's start by exploring insignificant itemizable deductions.

Insignificant Itemizable Deductions Example

Itemizable Deduction	**Amount ($)**
Charitable contributions	100
Medical expenses	1,000
Homeownership expenses	0
State and local taxes	1,400
Total ($)	**2,500**

As the table above shows, your itemizable deductions total $2,500. For this scenario, imagine you: (i) are single; (ii) rent an apartment; and (iii) have low medical expenses and charitable contributions.

If you choose to use your itemized deductions of $2,500 your taxable income will be $52,500 ($55,000 - $2,500). Choosing to itemize your deductions causes your taxable income to be higher by $9,900 ($52,500 - $42,600) than if you had chosen to use the standard deduction.

So if your goal is to pay the least tax possible, choose to use the standard deduction if your itemized deductions are lower than the standard deduction for your filing status. However, if your goal is to pay as much tax as possible, give me a call, because I would like to learn how you got so rich and wealthy.

Now let's explore an example where you have significant itemizable deductions. Again, let's assume you are single and have an annual salary of $55,000. But, now: (i) you own a home; (ii) incurred high medical expenses because you were seriously injured; and (iii) made substantial charitable contributions:

Significant Itemizable Deductions Example

Itemizable Deduction	**Amount ($)**
Charitable contributions	1,000
Medical expenses	3,000
Homeownership expenses	9,500
State and local taxes	1,500
Total ($)	**15,000**

As the table above shows, your itemizable deductions total $15,000. If you choose to use your itemized deductions of $15,000 your taxable income will be $40,000 ($55,000 - $15,000).

Choosing to itemize your deductions causes your taxable income to be lower by $2,600 ($40,000 - $42,600) than if you had decided to use the standard deduction. Thus, if your goal is to pay the least tax possible, you would choose to deduct your $15,000 of itemized deductions from your gross income instead of deducting your $12,400 standard deduction.

I feel obligated to emphasize I have vastly oversimplified deductions. For example, we did not distinguish between above and below the line deductions or real-world limitations to the selected, example itemizable deductions we explored. But for purposes of this book and developing an introductory, fundamental understanding of deductions, our discussion should suffice. Let's now cover: exemptions.

Exemptions

Exemptions are a reduction for each person covered by a tax return. People covered by a tax return include: (i) the taxpayer themselves; (ii) the taxpayer's spouse (if married, filing jointly); and (iii) dependents cared for by the taxpayer (for example, the taxpayer's children or elderly parents).

Let's begin exploring personal exemptions by again assuming your annual salary is $55,000. This time, however, also imagine: (i) it is 2017; (ii) you are married, filing jointly; and (iii) have two children. Why 2017? Well, in 2017 the federal personal exemption was $4,050.

Given the above assumptions, you would be eligible to claim four personal exemptions totaling $16,200 ($4,050 * 4 exemptions). Why four personal exemptions? You get one personal exemption for each of: (i) you; (ii) your spouse; (iii) and your two children (dependents).

Collectively, this results in taxable income of $38,800 ($55,000 - $16,200). However, changes to federal tax law in 2018 eliminated federal personal exemptions for 2018 and beyond. So for federal tax purposes, personal exemptions no longer exist.

But remember, you have to file at least two tax returns each year you earn income, one tax return for each of: (i) federal and (ii) every state in which you earned income. And because each state has their own tax law, personal exemptions generally still exist for state tax returns.

Remember those 75,000 pages of tax rules? Well, those are just the federal tax rules! *Each* state has tens of thousands of additional pages of their own tax rules. Sigh. We are now ready to explore tax brackets by leveraging our understanding of: gross income, reductions, and taxable income.

Tax Brackets

Gross Tax Owed Formula

Gross tax owed = Taxable income * Brackets

Your gross tax owed depends on your taxable income and the tax brackets applicable to your taxable income. As we have already discussed, taxable income is calculated by subtracting reductions from gross income (TI = GI - R).

Tax brackets are: (i) determined by tax law; (ii) generally revised every year; and (iii) unique per filing status. Conceptually, tax brackets consist of two components: (i) tax rates and (ii) taxable income ranges. To better understand tax brackets, let's explore the federal tax brackets for taxpayers filing single in 2020:

2020 Federal Income Tax Brackets, Filing Single

Tax Rate (%)	Taxable Income ($)		
10	0	to	9,525
12	9,526	to	38,700
22	38,701	to	82,500
24	82,501	to	157,500
32	157,501	to	200,000
35	200,001	to	500,000
37	500,001	to	Infinity

As the table above shows, each **tax bracket** includes a: (i) tax rate and (ii) taxable income range. Each taxable income range has a floor and ceiling. For example, the 10% tax bracket has a taxable income floor of $0 and ceiling of $9,525.

It is a common misconception the gross tax you owe is a single tax rate multiplied by your taxable income. Let's debunk this misconception. Assume like before, your gross income earned from an annual salary is $55,000.

Further, assume your filing status is single and you choose to use the federal standard deduction. These assumptions result in taxable income of $42,600 ($55,000 - $12,400). If this common single tax rate misconception were true, your gross tax owed would be $9,372 ($42,600 * 22%). Why 22%? Because your taxable income is within the 22% taxable income range.

Thankfully for you and your bank account balance, this is *not* how tax brackets work. But unfortunately for your learning curve, tax brackets are slightly more complicated. But I know you are capable of learning tax brackets because you have made it this far. So, chin up, shoulders back! Let's continue.

The first step to fully understanding tax brackets is to understand: any single tax rate applies only to your taxable income *within* the taxable income range of the same row. To correctly calculate your total gross tax owed, add together the gross tax owed from each applicable tax bracket. Let's walk through this step by step.

The first step is determining which tax brackets are relevant to you. Any tax bracket is relevant to you if its floor is less than your total taxable income. Meaning, the first three tax brackets are relevant to you because your taxable income is $42,600. The second step is calculating the tax owed for each tax bracket as I have demonstrated in the following table:

Total Gross Tax Owed

Tax Rate (%)	Taxable Income ($)			Tax Owed ($)
10	0	to	9,525	925
12	9,526	to	38,700	3,501
22	38,701	to	82,500	858
			Total ($)	**5,312**

As shown in the table above, your total gross tax owed will be $5,312. Remember, your taxable income was only $42,600 ($55,000 - $12,400). Take a moment and appreciate just how much lower your correctly calculated total gross tax owed of $5,312 is compared to the total gross tax owed of $9,372 we incorrectly calculated using the common single tax rate misconception.

At first glance, the values in the last column of the table above might feel wrong. How can your tax owed in the 22% tax bracket be less than your combined tax owed from both the 10% and 12% tax brackets? What gives? Hopefully, you recall any single tax rate applies only to your taxable income within the taxable income range of the same row.

For example, only your taxable income between $0 and $9,525 is taxed at 10%. Only your taxable income between $9,525 and $38,700 is taxed at 12%. And finally, only your taxable income between $38,700 and $42,600 is taxed at 22%.

Resultantly, you only have $3,900 ($42,600 - $38,700) of taxable income in the 22% tax bracket. This means only $3,900 of your taxable income is taxed at 22%. Thus, your tax owed for the 22% tax bracket is only $858 ($3,900 * 22%).

And to reiterate, adding together all gross tax owed for each individual tax bracket calculation provides us with our total gross tax owed. Having covered gross tax owed, we can move on to: tax credits.

Credits

Net Tax Owed Formula

Net tax owed = Gross tax owed - Credits

Similar to reductions, credits reduce the tax you owe. However, unlike reductions which reduce your gross income, credits reduce your gross tax owed. Interestingly enough, some credits are refundable and can reduce your gross tax owed to a negative number, resulting in a tax refund.

For example, if your gross tax owed was $2,000 but you qualified for a *refundable* $3,000 credit, the government would pay you $1,000! Comparatively, if this $3,000 credit were instead *non-refundable*, then your net tax owed would simply be $0.

While we will not cover specific tax credits in detail, common tax credits in 2020 involve: foreign earned income, education, and dependents. For our purposes, just know: (i) tax credits reduce gross tax owed and result in net tax owed and (ii) net tax owed is the amount of tax you are legally obligated to pay your government when you file your tax return.

Refund

As just alluded to (the government paying you $1,000) when discussing tax credits, there is something called a tax refund. For a variety of reasons, the government may owe you money when you file your tax return, which is called a **tax refund**.

Perhaps the most common reason a taxpayer might receive a tax refund is because they overpaid their estimated tax owed throughout the year. Estimated tax owed? What?

Yup, you owe your government estimated tax payments throughout the year. Thus, your employer withholds (and pays the government) some of your income from each paycheck at a rate resulting in withholding an estimated amount of tax you will owe on your tax return. Additionally, if you are self-employed, you are responsible for making estimated tax payments every three months.

Given this tax withholding is an estimate, only upon completing and filing your tax return do you and the government know exactly how much net tax you owe (or refund you are entitled to). For example, let's continue to use your annual salary assumption of $55,000 along with the assumption you have no tax credits.

Let's further assume your employer withheld $7,000 throughout the entire tax year. Further, recall we already determined your net tax owed is $5,312 ($5,312 gross tax - $0 credits). This means you would be entitled to a tax refund of $1,688 ($7,000 - $5,312). Conversely, if (for example) your employer has withheld only $4,000 instead of $7,000 you would owe the government $1,312 ($5,312 - $4,000).

Do It Yourself: Tax Calculator

For those interested in exploring earned income taxation further, use ~~Bing~~ your favorite search engine to search for: "tax calculator." Alternatively, you can use the tax calculator I built for readers of this book at: **https://www.fundamental.finance/tax-calculator/**

My tax calculator has capabilities not generally available in the other tax calculators your favorite search engine will show you. Regardless which tax calculator you decide to use, I am confident you will benefit from further exploring taxes on your own with a calculator.

Conclusion

I will be brief because we have probably already talked more about taxes than you signed up for. To recap, net tax owed is: (i) gross income minus reductions; (ii) multiplied by tax brackets; (iii) minus credits. Now that we are earned income tax experts (lul), we will explore: unearned income taxes.

Unearned Income Taxes

Introduction

We have already learned income earned from *working* is called: earned income. Remember all those 40 to 50 hour work weeks you dragged yourself through? Only to have your government (through taxes) rob you of 20% to 30% of all your earned income?!

Remember the lifestyle I have been mentioning throughout this book? "Investing," you accurately conjure. Yay, you remembered! As a refresher, investing is: putting your savings to work for you.

And if you recall, investors seek two rewards: (i) appreciation and (ii) income. And although one investing reward is actually called income, both investing income and appreciation are **unearned income** for tax purposes.

The *unearned* part of unearned income is fitting because *you* did not earn this income, your *investments* earned this income. And like earned income, unearned income is also taxed. Let's begin to explore unearned income taxation by discussing: capital assets.

Capital Asset

Virtually everything you own (for tax purposes) is considered a **capital asset**. Yes, everything, including: the new flat-screen television you just bought; your clothes, jewelry, and home; any stocks, bonds, or other investments you own; and, well, *everything*! And in order for anyone to own something, someone (either you or whoever gave the thing to you) purchased the thing at some point, which brings us to: cost basis.

Cost Basis

When you buy a capital asset, you establish its cost basis. **Cost basis** (initially) is the price you pay for the capital asset. But your cost basis includes not only your purchase price, but also additional costs you incur to acquire or improve the capital asset, including: sales tax, shipping and handling, commissions, fees, and installation costs.

Additionally, your cost basis can be reduced over time, most commonly by an accounting concept called: depreciation. However, a discussion about depreciation is beyond the scope of this book.

For our purposes, just know your cost basis is related to: (i) the sales price you paid to acquire a capital asset and (ii) includes more than just the sales price. If cost basis is all about purchasing capital assets, selling capital assets is all about: capital return.

Capital Return

Capital Return Formula

Capital return = Sales price - Cost basis

When you sell a capital asset, the difference between your cost basis and sales price will create a capital gain or a capital loss, which we will collectively refer to as: **capital return**. Thus, there are two types of capital returns, capital: (i) gain and (ii) loss.

A **capital gain** occurs when your sales price is greater than your cost basis, while a **capital loss** occurs when your sales price is lower than your cost basis. Thus, a positive capital return is capital gain, and a negative capital return is a capital loss.

If you recall from the beginning of this book, we discussed the two rewards investors seek: (i) appreciation and (ii) income. Each of these rewards are unearned income, and taxed slightly differently. We will start with appreciation, which is synonymous with capital gain and loss.

Similar to the taxation of earned income, most tax authorities tax capital gains. However, most tax authorities tax capital gains at different tax rates (usually lower) than earned income, making unearned income **tax-advantaged**.

Advocates of this reduced-rate policy believe lower tax rates: (i) incentivize citizens to invest and (ii) should be lower because investments are purchased with earned income that has already been taxed.

While critics believe this reduced-rate policy unfairly benefits investors and unfairly burdens people who choose to spend all their income on expenses instead of saving and investing. But regardless your opinion of investment taxation, unearned income *is* taxed.

Realized capital returns are to earned income what taxable income is to earned income. The key word here is *realized* capital returns. A **realized capital return** is an *actual* capital return from an *actual* sale of a capital asset. Conversely, an **unrealized capital return** is the hypothetical capital return you would realize *if* you sold your capital asset.

Thankfully tax authorities do not tax unrealized capital gains (which makes sense, given no actual sale occurred). However, realized capital returns (gains and losses) are taxed. We will start with: realized capital gains.

Capital Gain

Let's work through capital gains in detail. For example, imagine you purchased ten shares of stock for a price of $50 per share, and paid your broker a $6 commission to conduct the transaction.

Recall the beginning of this chapter for a moment. We learned your cost basis is sales price plus related costs. So in our example, your sales price is $500 (10 shares * $50 per share) plus a related cost of $6 (broker commission). Thus, your total cost basis is $506 ($500 + $6), or $50.60 per share ($506 / 10 shares).

Let's further agree you will: (i) sell all ten of your shares and (ii) will be charged a $6 commission by your broker to sell all ten shares. The $6 commission required sales commission can be added to your cost basis, meaning your total cost basis becomes $512 ($506 + $6), or $51.20 per share ($512 / 10 shares).

Resultantly, you would have to sell your ten shares for more than $51.20 per share to realize any capital gains. So, if you sell all ten shares of your stock for $55 each, you will realize a total capital gain of $38 ($550 - $512), or $3.80 per share ($55 - $51.20).

We will cover how capital gains impact tax owed later in this chapter. For now, let's move on to: capital loss.

Capital Loss

But what if you sell your ten shares of stock for $50 per share instead of $55 per share? As mentioned previously, selling a capital asset for less than your cost basis results in a capital loss. Let's explore.

In this scenario, you will receive $500 ($50 * 10 shares) from selling your ten shares of stock, and again have a total cost basis of $512 ($500 + $6 + $6). This means when you sell your shares you will realize a total capital loss of $12 ($512 - $500), or $1.20 per share ($51.20 - $50).

We will cover how capital losses impact tax owed later in this chapter. As experts on the basics of capital returns (gains and losses), we can now look at: investment income.

Income

In addition to the taxation of investment appreciation, investment income is also taxed. Common types of investment income include: dividends, interest, premiums, and rent. **Dividends** are income from stocks. **Interest** is income from bonds and currency in bank accounts. **Premiums** are income from options. **Rent** is income from real estate.

Importantly, each type of investment income is taxed differently depending on: (i) the type of income (for example, dividends versus premiums) and (ii) the type of investment account (for example, brokerage versus retirement).

However, a detailed discussion of the taxation difference between various types of investment income is beyond the scope of this book. All you need to know for now is investment (unearned) income is usually taxed at lower rates than earned income. We will, however, spend some time exploring investment accounts and their respective taxation.

Investment Account Taxation

Hopefully, every reader is reasonably familiar with the concept of traditional saving and checking bank accounts. These bank accounts hold currency deposited into them. The equivalent of these bank accounts for investments are: brokerage accounts.

Bank accounts can only hold currency, while brokerage accounts can hold both currency *and* investments. Saving and checking accounts are standard bank accounts, while brokerage accounts are standard investment accounts. However, only with a brokerage (or other investment) account can you use the currency you deposited to purchase investments.

Any interest income you earn from your bank on currency in your saving, checking, and brokerage account is unearned income. Additionally, all income and capital returns earned from your investments are unearned income. And like earned income, unearned income is also taxed. Thankfully, there are special investment accounts you can use to avoid or delay unearned income taxes.

These special investment accounts are known as **tax-advantaged**. With a brief introduction on investment account taxation behind us, we can explore tax-advantages of specific (yet to be mentioned) investment accounts, based on: (i) time and (ii) subject matter. But before we cover tax-advantaged accounts, we need to briefly cover: deposits and withdrawals.

Deposits And Withdrawals

In order to explain withdrawals, let's first define: deposits. A **deposit** occurs when you put currency into your bank account or investment account, while a **withdrawal** occurs when you remove currency from your account(s).

There are virtually no limitations regarding deposits or withdrawals in saving, checking, and brokerage accounts. Account owners can deposit and withdraw as much currency as they want, as frequently as they want, and can spend withdrawn currency on whatever they please.

No deposit or withdrawal is *itself* taxed. Tax is owed only on unearned income generated within these accounts. For example, interest income in your bank account and investment income or capital returns in your brokerage account.

Comparatively, tax-advantaged accounts have many limitations regarding deposits and withdrawals. First, most tax-advantaged accounts restrict how much currency can be deposited into the account each year. As we will explore later in this chapter, deposit limitations are controlled by (and even amongst) the subject matter of the tax-advantage.

Second, similar to deposits, many tax-advantaged accounts have restrictions regarding withdrawals. However, unlike deposit limitations which restrict how much currency can be deposited, withdrawal limitations are more based on: time and use.

Note, withdrawal of *deposits* is usually unrestricted, meaning: withdrawal restrictions generally only affect withdrawals of capital returns. For example, retirement investment accounts often penalize and tax withdrawals of capital returns prior to retirement.

Finally, certain tax-advantaged accounts penalize and tax withdrawals used for unpermitted purposes. For example, education or health investment accounts restrict the use of withdrawals to paying for, respectively, education or health expenses. Comparatively, retirement investment account withdrawals can be used for any purpose.

Having completed an overview of deposits and withdrawals, we are now ready to begin our discussion of: time-based tax-advantaged accounts.

Time-Based Tax-Advantaged Accounts

Time-based tax-advantaged accounts can be divided into two categories based on when a taxpayer owes tax related to these accounts. The two time-based categories are: (i) pre-tax (known as "traditional") and (ii) post-tax (known as "roth").

Both pre and post tax-advantaged accounts enable taxpayers to avoid owing unearned income tax *between the time* when currency is: (i) deposited into (ii) and withdrawn from the account. This alone is a tax-advantage over brokerage accounts because all capital return and investment income earned in a brokerage account is taxed.

However, there are additional, but differing tax-advantages over brokerage accounts. **Pre tax-advantaged** accounts enable taxpayers to exclude from gross income the earned income *deposited* into pre tax-advantaged accounts. However, any unearned income withdrawn from a pre tax-advantaged account is taxed at the applicable *earned* income tax rate and bracket *at the time of withdrawal.*

Post tax-advantaged accounts enable taxpayers to exclude from gross income the earned income *withdrawn* from the post tax-advantaged account. However, no capital gain or investment income withdrawn from a post tax-advantaged account is ever taxed. Thus, the advantage of a post tax-advantaged account is withdrawals *are not taxed at all.*

Resultantly, investors use pre tax-advantaged accounts if they believe their current earned income will be taxed at higher rates than future withdrawals from the account. However, this is somewhat of a guessing game because, hopefully you remember, tax rules, rates, and brackets change over time.

Subject Matter Tax-Advantaged Accounts

Tax-advantaged accounts can also be broadly categorized based on the subject matter they advantage. The three tax-advantaged subjects we will cover involve: (i) education; (ii) health; and (iii) retirement.

Education

Two common **education tax-advantaged accounts** are: (i) 529 plans and (ii) education savings accounts (ESA). Both 529s and ESAs are post tax-advantaged accounts. Thus, no unearned income is taxed inside either account or upon withdrawal.

Currency withdrawn from education tax-advantaged accounts can only be used for specific education expenses permitted by tax law. Withdrawals used for any non-education purpose lose their tax-advantaged status, resulting in withdrawal penalties and tax owed on any unearned income withdrawn.

Health

Two common **health tax-advantaged accounts** are: (i) flexible spending accounts (FSA) and (ii) health savings accounts (HSA). Both FSAs and HSAs are pre tax-advantaged accounts. Thus, no unearned income is taxed inside either account, but is taxed upon withdrawal.

Currency withdrawn from health tax-advantaged accounts can only be used for specific health expenses permitted by tax law. Withdrawals used for any non-health purpose lose their tax-advantaged status, resulting in withdrawal penalties and tax owed on any unearned income withdrawn.

Importantly, any unspent currency in an FSA at the end of the year is forfeited. Yes, you read that right. Use it, or lose it. Who gets the unspent currency? Your employer. Moreover, no investments can be purchased and held in FSAs.

Resultantly, FSAs are basically just tax-advantaged checking accounts with a use it or lose it penalty. And because of FSA's use it or lose it penalty, much like revolvers to Matthew Quigley, "I never had much use for one."

Comparatively, unspent balances in HSAs are not forfeited and remain in your HSA until withdrawn. Additionally, unlike FSAs which can only hold currency, investments can be purchased in HSAs. Finally, the most unique characteristic of HSAs is (as of 2020): HSAs are the *only* tax-advantaged account both pre *and* post tax-advantaged.

Retirement

Retirement tax-advantaged accounts can be broadly categorized by: (i) employer sponsorship or (ii) individual ownership. Employer-sponsored retirement accounts are maintained by employers for employees. Conversely, individual retirement accounts are maintained by individual taxpayers independent of any employment.

Two common types of **employer-sponsored retirement accounts** are: (i) 401(k)s and (ii) 403(b)s. For our purposes, 401(k)s and 403(b)s are virtually identical, as both are: retirement accounts employers make available to employees. The only difference we will cover here is *which* employers can offer which employer-sponsored retirement account(s).

The only employers who can provide 403(b) include: schools, government organizations, religious entities, and other not-for-profit organizations. Although we have only mentioned 401(k)s and 403(b)s this far, we will briefly mention two more 403(b) equivalents: (i) 457s and (ii) thrift saving plans.

Public service employees (for example, police officers or firefighters) often have 457s, while federal government employees and military personnel often have thrift saving plans. So, in summary, 403(b)s, 457s, and thrift saving plans are limited to specific types of employers and employees.

Comparatively, any employer can provide employees with a 401(k). But because of a variety of tax-advantages 403(b)s and equivalents have over 401(k)s (all of which are beyond the scope of this book): most employers who qualify to offer 403(b)s choose to provide 403(b)s instead of 401(k)s. This means 401(k)s are generally only provided by for profit employers (meaning, any regular, degular corporation).

The two most common types of **individual retirement accounts (IRA)** are: (i) traditional and (ii) roth. If you recall, we introduced pre and post tax-advantages and mentioned "traditional" meant pre-tax, while "roth" meant post-tax. As you might imply from their names, the primary difference between traditional and roth IRAs is their pre (traditional) and post (roth) tax-advantage.

However, there are many additional types of IRAs, including: nondeductible, self-directed, spousal, simplified employee pension (SEP), and savings incentive match plan for employees (SIMPLE). Though, a detailed discussion of each additional IRA type is beyond the scope of this book.

Alright, great success! With a sufficient exploration of investment account taxation basics behind us, we are now ready to explore: tax owed on unearned income.

Tax Owed

Alright, so far we know no tax is owed for capital returns or investment income (collectively, unearned income) if: (i) unrealized or (ii) in a tax-advantaged account. Further, we have already covered no tax is owed for withdrawals from post tax-advantaged accounts, while withdrawals from pre tax-advantaged accounts are considered earned income.

Phew! Let's simplify. Combining everything from the previous paragraph results in unearned income tax owed only for: (i) realized capital gains and investment income (ii) in traditional brokerage accounts.

Remember, any unearned income withdrawn from pre tax-advantaged accounts is taxed at earned income tax rates and brackets. To begin our exploration of taxable unearned income, we will briefly introduce two important concepts: (i) holding period and (ii) netting.

Your **holding period** is the length of time you owned a capital asset. Thus, each capital asset you own has its own holding period. Holding periods are separated into two timeframes: (i) short or (ii) long. **Short-term** means "one year or less," while **long-term** means "more than one year," or more technically, "a year and one day."

Importantly, all capital returns are "netted" every year. While technically nuanced, we will keep things simple and define **netting** as: the summation of an entire year's short-term capital returns and long-term capital returns (collectively, capital activity).

You see, in a single tax year you might have both short-term capital returns and long-term capital returns. For example, you might have: (i) short-term capital gains of $100; (ii) short-term capital losses of $600; and (iii) long-term capital gains of $1,500. The sum (netting) of these capital returns is: net long-term capital gains of $1,000 ($100 - $600 + $1,000).

Admittedly, our $1,000 capital activity netting example is jejune. Netting is more complicated in real life because of annual loss limitations and resulting carryover. But these more intricate nuances aren't important for our purposes. Just know capital activity is netted for calculating tax owed.

Most tax authorities tax net short-term capital gains at the same tax rates as earned income, but tax net long-term capital gains and investment income at rates lower than earned income rates.

2020 Unearned Income Tax Brackets, Filing Single

Tax Rate (%)	Taxable Income ($)		
0	0	to	40,000
15	40,001	to	441,450
20	441,451	to	Infinity

The table above shows the 2020 unearned income tax brackets for federal taxpayers filing single (remember, net short-term unearned income is taxed as earned income. Calculating tax owed for unearned income is virtually identical to calculating tax owed for earned income, but with two added complexities.

First, net short-term unearned income is treated just like earned income (included in gross income and taxed according to the tax rate and brackets covered previously). The only complexity here is net short-term capital losses reduce gross income (much like a reduction), while net short-term unearned income increases gross income.

The second complexity involves net long-term unearned income. For tax rate and bracket purposes, net long-term unearned income is added to taxable income, not gross income. Let's explore.

For discussion purposes, recall our jejune $1,000 net long-term unearned income example. As the table below shows, your taxable net long-term unearned income (and unearned income tax owed) depends on: (i) your taxable earned income and (ii) the long-term unearned income tax bracket table above.

Unearned Income Tax Owed

Taxable Earned Income ($)	Taxable Unearned Income ($)	Unearned Income Tax Owed ($)
39,000	0	0
39,500	500	75
40,000	1,000	150

But let's go one level deeper and imagine yourself several decades from now as: an experienced, high value-creating professional and lifelong investor. Let's suppose you: (i) are single; (ii) have taxable earned income of $400,000; and (iii) have net long-term unearned income of $100,000.

Based on the 2020 unearned income tax brackets for taxpayers filing single, your unearned income tax owed would be $17,928 (consisting of $41,500 net-long-term unearned income taxed at 15% and $58,550 taxed at 20%). Were your $100,000 net long-term unearned income taxed at 2020 earned income tax rates, your unearned income tax owed would nearly double to $35,000!

Your Home

The single most expensive capital asset many people will ever buy is their home. Fortunately, most tax authorities allow you to exclude some, or all, capital gain from the sale of your home as long as you meet certain requirements.

In America, as of 2020, you can exclude realized capital gain from the sale of your home of up to: (i) $250,000 if you are single and (ii) $500,000 if you are married, filing jointly. However, as previously stated, there are certain requirements taxpayers must meet to be eligible to exclude this capital gain.

The requirements are: (i) for at least two years (aggregately, not consecutively) out of the five years prior to the sale you (ii) owned the house; (iii) used the house as your primary residence; and (iv) you have not excluded any capital gain from a previous home sale in the two-year period immediately before the current sale.

Phew. That was a mouthful. Let's try that again, but this time in plain English. You are able to exclude $250,000 to $500,000 of realized capital gain from the sale of your home if you: (i) owned your home; (ii) lived in your home for at least 730 days (two years) of the last 1,826 days (five years); and (iii) have not used this exclusion in the last two tax years.

Conclusion

The main takeaways from our discussion in this chapter are unearned income tax owed depends on the type of: (i) unearned income (capital gain versus investment income); (ii) holding period (short-term versus long-term); and (iii) investment account (brokerage versus tax-advantaged).

Debt

Introduction

Much earlier in this book, we learned how investing is compounding that works *for* you. In this chapter, we will discuss, among other things, how debt is compounding that works *against* you and *for* someone else. You read that right. Against you. Let this sink in. But let's be more specific. **Debt** is currency borrowed *by* one person *from* another person.

Regardless the type of debt, all debt is currency: (i) borrowed by you (making you a "borrower" or "debtor") and (ii) loaned by someone else (making them a "lender" or "creditor"). Many financial professionals recommend you not borrow from, or lend to, friends or family. So in this chapter we will presume you are borrowing from a: (i) bank; (ii) business; or (iii) government.

Key Concepts

There are many types of debt. For example, when you purchase a car using debt, you are "financing" your vehicle. When you buy something with your credit card, you are using debt called "credit" (hence "credit card"). When you pay for college using debt, you are using a "loan" (hence "student loan"). And when you purchase a home using debt, you are using a "loan" (hence "home loan").

Before we discuss specific types of debt, let's explore debt's most fundamental general concepts, starting with: principal.

Principal

The initial amount of currency you borrow is known as **principal**. For example, if you borrow $20,000 to buy a car, your loan principal is $20,000. Relatedly, **origination** is when a lender gives you a loan by approving your request (application). So, you were able to borrow $20,000 to buy a car because a lender originated a $20,000 loan to you.

At any given point in time, any principal you still owe is called **outstanding principal**. On Day 1 when you buy your car, your loan principal and outstanding principal are both $20,000. But as we will explore later, you will be required to make monthly payments to your lender to repay your car loan.

So, let's imagine, for example, in two years from today, you have repaid $6,000 of principal. Accordingly, in two years, your outstanding principal will be $14,000 while your original loan principal of $20,000 remains unchanged. But understanding original and outstanding principal only gets us so far. As we will learn next, lenders require: principal be repaid within a specific timeframe (term).

Term

The duration of a loan is known as the **term** of the loan. For example: most car loans have a six-year term, most home loans have a 30-year term, and most education loans have a 10-year term.

Now, if you were to borrow $100 from your friends or family, you might promise to repay them $100 in say, 100 days from today. Your family and friends probably will not require you to repay them $1 each day, but instead be okay with you repaying them $100 in 100 days from today.

But, unlike friends and family, lenders require borrowers to make a monthly payment each month during the loan's term. However, before we discuss required monthly payments, let's revisit a concept introduced much earlier in this book: interest.

Interest

We explored investment interest much earlier in this book when first learning about APR and APY. Now we will learn about debt interest. We will begin exploring loan interest by oversimplifying: interest owed.

Interest owed to a lender by a borrower is calculated by multiplying a loan's APR by its outstanding principal. Now you might be tempted to think debt APR and APY are as straightforward as it is for investing. But as you might now have guessed, they are not. Let's dive into the details of debt APR by starting with some example assumptions.

Let's start off assuming you borrow $300,000 of principal for a 30-year term at a 4% APR. These assumptions reasonably represent a typical American home loan (in 2020) because the median home price in the United States is approximately $300,000 and most home loans have 30-year terms.

If calculating debt interest owed were straightforward, we could calculate annual interest owed by multiplying your APR by your principal, which in our example would total $12,000 ($300,000 * 4%). Now, you might be tempted to presume your required monthly payment equals $1,000 ($12,000 / 12 months).

But as you will see shortly, your required monthly payment for a 30-year, $300,000 home loan with a 4% APR is $1,432 per month. Why $1,432 and not $1,000? Because your lender requires payment each month of both principal and interest.

But what if your APR was not always 4%? What if your APR could change periodically? An APR that can change during your term is an **adjustable rate**, while an APR that does not change during the term of the loan is a **fixed rate**. To keep things simple though, for the rest of this chapter we will presume all APRs we discuss are fixed rate APRs.

Required Monthly Payment

As mentioned previously, repaying debt involves required monthly payments. **Required monthly payments** consist of principal and interest. As already mentioned, the required monthly payment for a 30-year, $300,000 home loan with a 4% APR is $1,432.

Now (based on our previously calculated annual interest owed of $1,000 per month), you might be tempted to conclude you are repaying principal of $432 per month if your required monthly payment is $1,432. And you would be right, but only for Month 1.

You see, in Month 2, your outstanding principal is no longer $300,000. Remember how you repaid $432 of principal in Month 1? Resultantly, your outstanding principal in Month 2 is $299,568. Thus, in Month 2 you only owe interest of $999 ($299,568 * 4% / 12 months), which means you repaid $433 of principal.

It is important you understand your required monthly payment remains constant at $1,432 per month. But the proportion of interest and principal repaid varies from month to month. This monthly recalculation of principal and interest owed is known as **amortization**.

We will not go any further into the nuances of amortization in this book. Just remember loans have required monthly payments consisting of: (i) principal repayment and (ii) interest owed.

Do It Yourself: Amortization Calculator

For those interested in exploring amortization further, use ~~DuckDuckGo~~ your favorite search engine to search for: "amortization calculator." Alternatively, you can use the amortization calculator I built for readers of this book at: **https://www.fundamental.finance/debtor-calculator/**

My amortization calculator has capabilities not generally available in the other amortization calculators your favorite search engine will show you. Regardless which amortization calculator you decide to use, I am confident you will benefit from further exploring amortization on your own with a calculator.

Common Types Of Debt

With a basic understanding of debt's key concepts behind us, we will now shift our focus to discussing common types of debt. And we will start with perhaps the most infamous type of debt: the credit card.

Credit Card

Like most topics these days (including credit cards): ask around, and you will receive no shortage of opinions. Some people think credit cards are amazing and should be used whenever possible. While other people swear credit cards are the embodiment of power evil. Feelings aside, the simple fact remains: credit cards are merely a tool, and their use or misuse cannot be blamed on the tool itself.

Physically, credit cards are rectangular pieces of plastic, with a magnetic strip across the back, and an RFID chip embedded in one end. *Functionally*, credit cards are swiped (magnetic strip) or inserted or tapped (RFID chip) into a payment machine to make a purchase. *Financially*, credit cards are a loan to you from a card issuer (more on card issuers later).

However, in the very near future, credit cards will likely completely cease to exist physically and functionally. We used to have to swipe credit cards (magnetic strips). Then we had to insert credit cards (RFID chip). Now we can tap to pay and save our credit card in our smartphone's wallet.

Why, in 2020, we still call this handheld device a smart*phone* is beyond me. We really should call this handheld device a smart*hand.* Which brings me to another futuristic prediction beyond credit card's impending extinction.

In recent decades, humans have been blurring the line between human and machine (known as **cybernetics**). We started with eyeglasses. We quickly moved on to replacing joints and bones with metal and material. Then we created hearing aids. Next was artificial hearts. And now, we have limb replacements called prosthetics.

I genuinely believe we will soon see people voluntarily replace their hands with advanced, smart prosthetics capable of everything smartphones are currently capable of. No more holding a device. All this functionality (and eventually much more) will be built into your smarthand!

I also cannot wait until I can replace my feet with prosthetics containing jet packs! Just imagine, no more foot pain after an entire day of walking because you can just jetpack around! Waow! But I digress. Where were we? Credit cards? Ah yes, credit cards.

Credit cards are revolving debt. Revolving debt is slightly different from the **fixed debt** we have discussed thus far, which has required monthly payments of a fixed amount consisting of both principal and interest.

Let's revisit your 30-year, $300,000 home loan with a 4% APR. As a fixed debt, your home loan requires you pay your lender exactly $1,432 each and every month for 30 years (for a total of 360 payments of $1,432). Your required monthly payment is fixed at $1,432 (hence fixed debt).

Now let's contrast fixed debt with the revolving debt of credit cards. First, you apply for a line of credit with a card issuer. A **card issuer** is a company which issues credit cards. The most common card issuers are perhaps: Visa, Mastercard, and American Express (but there are many more card issuers).

A card issuer will assess your creditworthiness (which we will cover in the next chapter) and either approve or deny your credit card application. If your credit card application is *denied*, consider applying for a secured credit card, which you can use to improve your creditworthiness (again, more on creditworthiness later).

If instead your credit card application is *approved*, you become a **cardholder**. However, your approval is conditioned by a credit limit. That is, the card issuer only approves (allows) you to spend (borrow) up to a certain amount (your credit limit) with your credit card.

Thus, your **credit limit** is the amount of revolving credit you are approved for. Your creditworthiness (which we will discuss in the next chapter) plays a substantial role is your: (i) approval and (ii) credit limit.

For our purposes, let's imagine your credit limit is $3,000. It is important to understand you do not receive $3,000 from the card issuer. Instead, you receive a credit card. You can then go from store to store, spending *up to* your credit limit of $3,000.

However, if you attempt to use your credit card for a purchase that (combined with all your previous purchases) would exceed your credit limit, the transaction will be declined. This is what is happening in all those television and movie scenes where the "rich" person gets all embarrassed when the cashier or waiter says, "I am sorry, but your card was declined."

So unlike your fixed home loan where you received $300,000 to purchase your home, your credit card has a credit limit you can borrow (spend) up to. Your **outstanding balance** is the amount you have borrowed (spent) using your credit card, while your **available balance** is your credit limit minus your outstanding balance.

Importantly, you can, at any time, repay your card issuer some or all of your outstanding balance. Though as we will now discuss, repaying your entire outstanding balance each month will prevent you from owing any interest to your card issuer, effectively making your credit card loan interest free!

Interest

Once a month, your card issuer will send you a bill equal to the total amount you spent (borrowed) that month. Credit card bills usually have 30-day terms, which means any payment you make within 30 days is considered on time, while any payment made after 30 days is considered late.

For our purposes, assume you spent $1,000 with your credit card in Month 1. Your card issuer will send you a bill for $1,000 and you will have 30 days (until the end of Month 2) to repay this $1,000. If you repay all $1,000 within 30 days, you will not be charged any interest!

You read that right. If you pay your monthly credit card bill in full and on time, you will not be charged any interest! However, your card issuer will charge you interest based on your average daily balance if you fail to make a full or timely payment of $1,000.

We could spend several pages exploring average daily balance (I know because I wrote them and then decided not to include them). But a detailed understanding of average daily balance is not important for our purposes.

What *is* important is you remember: you can completely avoid ever paying any credit card interest if you simply pay your monthly credit card bill in full and on time. If you fail to make your monthly payments in full and on time, you will end up owing much, much more than you originally borrowed.

Not repaying your entire outstanding balance each month is known as **carrying a balance**. Carrying an outstanding balance is an excellent example of how compounding works against you. Credit card APRs are so high (typically, 13% to 24%) that carrying a balance on your credit card is extremely expensive for you, and extremely lucrative to your card issuer.

Let's see just how lucrative you carrying an outstanding balance is for your card issuer. Let's reuse our assumption you spent $1,000 on your credit card and further assume your credit card has a 20% APR.

Finally, let's assume you never make a single payment for four years. In just four years, your $1,000 carried balance will have more than doubled to approximately $2,200! Or $22,000 if your carried balance was $10,000. Yikes!

As my grandpa would say, "that is what you get for all that fooling around business." Hopefully, you avoid choosing poorly like Walter Donovan in *Indiana Jones and the Last Crusade*, and you instead choose wisely by choosing to pay your monthly credit card bill in full and on time.

Fees

Now some of you might be wondering how card issuers would stay in business if, hypothetically, no cardholder ever paid any credit card interest because they always paid their monthly credit card bill in full and on time.

This is unfortunately purely hypothetical because too many people fail, or are unable, to pay their credit card bill in full and on time. However, even if every cardholder always paid their outstanding balance in full and on time, card issuers would remain in business because of two credit card fees: (i) merchant and (ii) cardholder.

Credit card issuers charge businesses you purchase from a fee to accept your credit card. This fee credit card issuers charge businesses is called a **merchant fee**. This fee (as of 2020) is 2.9% and $0.29 per transaction for Visa and Mastercard, and even more for American Express. This is why you often see signs in smaller businesses saying something like, "minimum purchase with card: $5" or "$0.50 transaction fee with card."

Moreover, not all credit cards are free to own and use. Many credit cards charge cardholders a **foreign transaction fee** for any transaction conducted in a foreign currency (which would occur if you used your credit card while traveling abroad in a foreign country).

Further, some credit cards can also have fees for balance transfers, late payments, cash advances, and more. Some credit cards even have an **annual fee** cardholders must pay each year *just* to have the credit card! But credit cards with annual fees usually provide cardholders with incentive(s) that exceed the annual fee. These incentive(s) are known as: rewards.

Rewards

With the risk of owing interest and being charged fees, you might be wondering why anyone would ever use a credit card. Two common reasons include: (i) convenience (many people consider transacting with physical currency too cumbersome) and (ii) rewards (though not all credit cards have rewards).

The first type of credit card reward cardholders may be entitled to is: a sign-up bonus. A **sign-up bonus** is a one-time reward and often requires the cardholder to spend a minimum amount using the credit card in the first few months.

For example, a credit card might have a $300 sign-up bonus if you spend at least $3,000 on the credit card during the first three months you have the credit card. Assuming you do in fact spend at least $3,000 in the first three months, your card issuer will either: (i) reduce your outstanding balance by $300 or (ii) deposit $300 into your bank account.

In addition to a sign-up bonus, the other type of credit card reward cardholders may be entitled to is: use rewards. Unlike a one-time sign-up bonus, use rewards are perpetual. That is, **use rewards** are obtained indefinitely for each dollar you spend using your credit card.

There are two characteristics of use rewards: (i) quantity and (ii) type. We will start with: quantity. The quantity of reward you receive when you use your credit card takes one of three forms: (i) flat rate; (ii) tiered rate; or (iii) preferred merchant. We will start with: flat rate rewards.

Flat rate rewards provide cardholders with, for example, a 1% reward for every dollar spent. With a 1% reward, you would receive one reward for every $100 you spend using your credit card. For those wondering what one *thing* (reward) is rewarded, wonder not, all will be explained shortly when we discuss reward types.

Tiered rewards provide cardholders with a different reward quantity depending on the transaction category. For example, a credit card might provide (*for each dollar spent*): 3 rewards for dining transactions, 2 rewards for gas station transactions, and 1 reward for all other transaction types. Some credit cards even have a bonus category (periodically chosen by the card issuer or holder) which provides an extra bonus reward quantity for transactions within this rotating, periodic bonus category.

Preferred merchant rewards provide cardholders with rewards (or bonus rewards) when transacting with specific merchant(s). For example, you can obtain an Amazon credit card, with which you will receive a 5% reward whenever you purchase from Amazon, but only a 1% reward for any non-Amazon transaction.

With credit card reward quantities out of the way, we can now focus on credit card: reward types. There are three primary types of credit card rewards: (i) cash; (ii) points; and (iii) miles. We will start with: cash rewards.

Cash rewards provide cardholders with a cash reward based on their reward quantity. For example, if you have a flat rate 1% percent cash back reward credit card, you will receive a cash payment of $1 for every $100 you spend using your credit card.

Point-based rewards provide cardholders with points based on their reward quantity. For example, if you have a tiered rate point reward credit card, you might earn two points for any dining transaction and one point for any non-dining transaction.

Credit card points function virtually identically to tickets won at an arcade. At an arcade, you exchange the tickets you won for the prize(s) of your choosing the arcade has behind their prize counter. Similarly, credit card points may be exchanged for merchandise in your card issuer's proprietary, online shopping platform.

Mile-based rewards are similar to point-based rewards, typically rewarding one or two miles per dollar spent. These miles are essentially store credit that can be exchanged with a specific airline for discounted, free, or upgraded flights. For example, if you obtain an American Airlines credit card, you can exchange reward miles you accrue for American Airlines flight discounts.

Business

A **business loan** is, you guessed it, debt borrowed by businesses! Should be no surprise there. While businesses may borrow for many reasons, borrowing to grow a business is the reasoning for borrowing we will focus on.

Imagine you own and operate an ice cream parlor business with a single location. Let's assume your net income is $1,000 per month after subtracting from gross income all expenses and tax owed. Moreover, let's imagine you needed $24,000 to open this first location because you needed to buy equipment, ingredients, signage, decorations, uniforms, and more.

Before continuing, let's take a brief moment to celebrate for two reasons. First, you habitually paid yourself first and managed to save and invest $24,000! Amazing. And second, you accumulated enough intellectual capital (money) to open and operate an ice cream parlor! Well done. Well done indeed.

Let's continue. If you wanted to grow your business (by opening a second location) without borrowing, you would have to save your $1,000 net income per month for 24 months (two years) before you would save a second $24,000.

Growing a business without borrowing by saving your net income is **organic growth**. Alternatively, a business can grow by borrowing (known as **leveraged growth**). For example, instead of taking two years to grow organically, imagine your ice cream business borrowed $24,000 on Day 1. Combining this $24,000 loan with your $24,000 savings results in your business having $48,000 on Day 1, which enables you to open two locations on Day 1.

Let's further imagine each location will generate net income of $1,000 per month *but for* your $24,000 business loan's required monthly payment. Let's presume your required monthly payment is approximately $250 based on a 15-year, $24,000 business loan with a 10% APR. Resultantly, your total net income per month from both locations is $1,750 ($1,000 + $1,000 - $250).

Let's take a deep breath and keep going, we are almost done. By borrowing $24,000 on Day 1, your business will generate enough net income ($24,500) to open a third location in just 14 months ($1,750 * 14). And with three locations collectively generating net income of $2,750 per month, it will take only nine months to earn enough net income ($24,750) to open a fourth location ($2,750 * 9).

In 24 months with organic growth, you will have two locations which earned total net income of $24,000 ($1,000 * 24). Comparatively, in 24 months with leveraged growth, your business will have generated total net income of $49,250 ($24,500 in first 14 months + $24,750 in last 9 months).

Let's now contrast your operating results in Year 3 assuming you do not open any additional locations after Month 24. Organic growth would result in two locations generating total net income of $1,750 per month, or $21,000 per year. While leveraged growth would result in four locations generating total net income of $3,750 per month, or $45,000 per year.

Here, I feel compelled to digress to reveal an important taxation difference between business income and earned income. Without having explicitly stated this reality, people who work for their income: (i) earn income; (ii) pay taxes; (iii) and can spend, save, and invest any remaining income.

Businesses have a tax-advantage over earned income because businesses: (i) earn income; (ii) spend, save, and invest; (iii) and pay taxes on any remaining income. I encourage you to reread this and the previous paragraph at least a second time, and reflect on this difference for some time.

Personal

You can think of personal loans this way: home loans are for buying homes, vehicle loans are for buying vehicles, student loans are for paying for college, business loans are for growing businesses, and for everything else, there are credit cards or personal loans.

Personal loans are loans made to people. Borrowers can use a personal loan for whatever they want, from: paying off higher APR outstanding credit card balances, to covering unexpected emergency expenses, to paying for weddings or vacations.

Sometimes, it makes sense to obtain a personal loan instead of using a credit card because personal loans may have lower APRs than credit cards. For example, in 2020, typical personal loan APRs are between 4% to 35%, while typical credit card APRs are between 13% to 25%. However, your APR will depend on your creditworthiness (again, we will cover creditworthiness in the chapter).

Unlike business loans, which accelerate business income, personal loans do not increase your personal (earned or unearned) income. Instead, personal loans merely: (i) accelerate the date of your consumption and (ii) increase the total cost of your purchase because of interest owed for your personal loan.

The alternative to obtaining a personal loan (or worse yet, carrying an outstanding credit card balance) is to save and invest until you can outright pay for what you want to purchase. But whatever you do, please, please, PLEASE: do not use a payday loan, whose APRs are several *hundred* percent. *gulp*

Home

A comprehensive discussion of home loans could easily be a whole chapter, if not an entire book. Do just a few minutes of research on your own, and you will encounter no shortage of home loan concepts, including: down payment, points, closing costs, FHA, VA, PMI, LTV, mortgage, fixed and adjustable APR, and many, many more.

Thankfully Uncle ~~Ben~~ Doug will cut through the noise and discuss only the essential home loan concepts everyone should know. To begin our home loan discussion, we will emphasize the difference between: mortgages and home loans.

Most people use the terms "mortgage" and "home loan" interchangeably as if mortgage is synonymous with home loan; similar to how most people use "money" synonymously with "currency." However, despite often being used interchangeably, mortgages and home loans are two different (but related) concepts; identical to how money and currency are two different (but related) concepts.

A **home loan** is the debt you borrow from a lender to purchase a home, while a **mortgage** is a legal agreement you enter into with your home loan lender in which you agree your lender can sell your home if you do not make your required monthly payments in full and on time.

Resultantly, a mortgage collateralizes your home. **Collateral** is property you promise to give to your lender if you are unable to make your required monthly payments in full and on time. So, in the case of a home loan with a mortgage, your home is collateral.

Should you fail to make your required monthly payments in full and on time, you end up in **foreclosure**. So when you hear the term "foreclosure sale," that particular home is being sold by a lender after a borrower stopped making their required monthly payments in full and on time.

With mortgage and collateral out of the way, there are several additional home loan concepts worth covering. First, home loans often have a very long term compared to other types of debt. For example, most home loans have a 15-year or 30-year term, while car loans often have 6-year terms, and student loans typically have 10-year terms.

Second, home loans often require a significant down payment. A **down payment** is a one-time payment equal to a percentage of the value of your home. Most home loan lenders require a 20% down payment.

However, multiple government-sponsored home loan programs permit a much lower down payment. For example, the Federal Housing Administration (FHA) has a home loan program for low-income and first-time homebuyers, which permits down payments as low as 3.5%.

Let's explore down payments further by revisiting your $300,000 home loan. There are two important details here to appreciate. First, your home *loan* is for $300,000. And second, at this point, your home *purchase price* and *down payment* are unknown.

So far we only know your lender has approved you for a $300,000 home loan. To determine your purchase price, we will presume your lender required a 20% down payment (which again, is a standard down payment percentage).

Knowing your down payment was 20% enables us to conclude your $300,000 home loan equals 80% of your purchase price. In home loan speak, this means your loan to value (LTV) ratio is 80% ($300,000 / $375,000). Armed with this collective knowledge, we can determine your: (i) purchase price was $375,000 ($300,000 / 80%) and (ii) down payment was $75,000 ($375,000 * 20%).

Now for many readers, you probably do not have $75,000 in savings; "yet," as my aunt would say. Enter the FHA. With a 3.5% down payment, an FHA loan reduces your 20% down payment of $75,000 to just $13,125 ($375,000 * 3.5%). Regardless how much you have saved, a $13,125 down payment is much lower, and therefore more achievable for many borrowers, than a $75,000 down payment.

However, keep in mind, the lower your down payment, the more you will have to borrow. And borrowing more results in owing more interest over your loan term. For example, all else being equal (30-year term; purchase price of $375,000; and 4% APR), a down payment of only 3.5% results in you paying $44,469 of additional interest over your 30-year term compared to a 20% down payment.

In addition to the difference between traditional and FHA down payments, FHA loans also permit borrowers to have lower credit scores compared to traditional home loan lenders. Most home loan lenders require a credit score of 650 or higher, while borrowers with a credit score as low as a 500 can be approved for FHA loans. The following table compares traditional bank home loans with FHA loans:

Comparing Bank And FHA Home Loans

Feature	Bank	FHA
Minimum credit score	625	500
Minimum down payment	20%	3.5%
APRs	Lower	Higher

It is important to remember though, the required monthly payments for your home loan are just the beginning of the story. Owning a home includes many additional expenses. For example, homeowners owe their local government property taxes each year.

Property taxes are generally based on a percentage of your home's purchase price. For example, an annual property tax of 1% is a reasonable assumption. Meaning a $375,000 home would have a $3,750 annual property tax, or $313 per month.

Additionally, homeowners are responsible for their home's: (i) maintenance and (ii) improvement. For example, typical maintenance includes lawn care and fixing broken appliances. While typical improvement expenses might include a kitchen remodel or building a patio deck. As a renter, your landlord is responsible for maintenance and improvement, not you.

Some homeowners even owe a monthly fee to belong to a community. This monthly community fee is known as a homeowner association (HOA) fee, and can easily be *hundreds* of dollars per month. HOAs are often gated communities and HOA fees support the maintenance and improvement of shared community resources, including: utilities, security, gyms, pools, playgrounds, and more.

Education

For better or worse, in 2020, many high school graduates believe in order to to have a successful career they need to obtain an undergraduate degree, if not also a graduate degree. And while it is true people with college degrees on average earn more over their lifetime than high school graduates, college has become extremely expensive.

Though often perceived as an inferior education, trade schools require far less time to complete (often 18 months or less) and are much less expensive than four-year colleges.

Similarly shunned is community college. It makes no sense to me why people avoid community college (I did not) because the first two years of college are primarily general education classes, which are essentially repeating courses you just completed in high school.

Many people may benefit from attending a trade school or community college. However, the perceived social stigma deters many people from these logical and viable post high school educational options. This means plenty of people who may benefit more from not attending four-year college are, to their detriment, attending four-year college.

Comparing California College Semester Cost (2020)

College	Cost ($)
Community College (CC)	1,100
California State University (CSU)	5,700
University of California (UC)	12,500
Private (for example, Santa Clara University)	26,500

As the table above shows, community college is by far the least expensive college option. Compared to attending community college: (i) a CSU is 5.2 times more expensive; (ii) a UC is 11.4 times; and (iii) Santa Clara University (SCU) 24.1 times more expensive.

Should you make the financially sensible decision to attend a community college, you should consider completing the intersegmental general education transfer curriculum (IGETC) and a transfer admission guarantee (TAG).

Completing IGETC and a TAG will enable you to transfer (as a rising junior) into most CSUs and UCs, as well as some private universities. Using IGETC and a TAG results in you spending two years in community college and two years at four-year college you transfer into, and ultimately graduate from.

Total Savings From Attending Community College

College	Savings ($)
CSU	18,400
UC	45,600
SCU	101,600

As the table above shows, choosing to attend community college for two years results in you saving no less than $18,400 (CSU) and up to $101,600 (SCU). Surely the general education english, math, and history courses are absolutely not worth $18,400 much less $101,600 (which let me again remind you, you *just* completed *for free* in high school).

But wait, there is more! We have not yet talked about grants, scholarships, or student loans. Your college financial aid office will have a list of available grants and scholarships, as well as help you obtain student loans. But we will start with grants and scholarships because they are similar in so much as neither is a loan.

Grants and scholarships are financial aid (gifts) you do not have to repay as long as you fulfill whatever eligibility requirement(s) might exist (which could be based on income thresholds, enrollment status, or academic performance).

Grants generally come from the government, while scholarships usually come from individuals or organizations.

For example, one of the grants offered by the United States federal government is the Pell Grant, which can be up to nearly $6,350 per year. Similarly, Cal Grants are provided by the State of California, which (depending on the type of college you are attending, for example, CC versus UC) can be worth more than $12,500 per year.

Comparatively, scholarship applications often have special requirements, unlike obtaining government grants, which involves little more than completing (each year) the free application for federal student aid (FAFSA). For example, scholarships often: (i) require you submit an essay and (ii) have specific eligibility criteria (for example, you must be pursuing a specific major).

With a basic grasp of grants and scholarships, we now can discuss student loans. **Student loans** are used to pay for educational expenses, including: tuition, housing, books, and fees.

While you can obtain private student loans to pay for college, the vast majority (more than 90%) of all outstanding student loan debt has been originated by the United States Department of Education. As of March 2020, approximately 32 million borrowers owed the United States Department of Education more than $1.2 trillion ($1,200,000,000,000).

Like home loans, student loans are also fixed debt. However, there are a few differences we will cover. First, is the number of loans. With a home loan, there is only ever one loan originated when you purchase your home (for simplicity, we are ignoring the possibility of any subsequent refinancing or home equity loan).

Comparatively, with student loans there is a new, separate loan originated each semester. For example, an undergraduate student who obtains a student loan each semester will have eight different student loans when they graduate. The second difference we will cover is: required monthly payments.

With a home loan (and fixed debt generally), you immediately become responsible for making required monthly payments one month after borrowing. With student loans, you are not obligated to make any required monthly payment until up to six months after you graduate.

This potential delay in required monthly payments is called **deferment**. Deferment is the earlier of: (i) six months after graduation or (ii) if you choose to start repaying earlier than six months after graduation.

Though, as we will explore in depth in just a moment, the longer you defer your required monthly payments, the more principal and interest you may end up owing your lender. Also, most student loans have a 10-year term, which begins when deferment ends.

The final difference is: interest. With a home loan, interest is regularly repaid with each required monthly payment. With student loans and deferment, interest still accrues based on the outstanding principal.

Any unpaid interest is capitalized at the end of deferment. **Capitalization** is the conversion of unpaid interest into additional principal owed. To fully explore capitalization, we must first explore student loan interest accrual. For starters, imagine you borrowed $10,000 each semester for four years with the following APRs:

Each Student Loan With APRs

Semester	**Loan ($)**	**APR (%)**
Freshman 1	10,000	7.0
Freshman 2	10,000	6.5
Sophomore 1	10,000	6.0
Sophomore 2	10,000	5.5
Junior 1	10,000	6.0
Junior 1	10,000	5.5
Senior 1	10,000	4.5
Senior 2	10,000	5.0
Total	**80,000**	**5.8**

As the table above shows, upon graduation you will have eight $10,000 student loans outstanding with a 5.8% weighted average APR. Importantly, you were being charged interest on your outstanding principal despite being able to defer making required monthly payments while you were a student. But because you deferred making any required monthly payments, the interest you were being charged went unpaid, and accrued.

Accrued Interest Formula

$$\text{Accrued interest} = P * (1 + APR / 365)\hat{}(365 * M / 12) - P$$

Accrued interest is the accumulation of owed, but unpaid, interest. Now let's walk through this accrued interest formula step-by-step, calculating the accrued interest for your Freshman 1 loan assuming you wait to make your first required monthly payment until the end of deferment (six months after graduation; 54 months since origination):

Accrued Interest Components

Abbreviation	Name	Value
P	Principal	$10,000
APR	APR	7%
M	Months	54

Accrued Interest Step-By-Step

Step	Result
Step 1	P * (1 + APR / 365)^(365 * M / 12) - P
Step 2	$10,000 * (1 + 7% / 365)^(365 / 54 / 12) - $10,000
Step 3	$10,000 * 1.0002^1,460 - $10,000
Step 4	$10,000 * 1.3702 - $10,000
Step 5	$13,702 - $10,000
Total ($)	**3,702**

As the table above shows, $3,702 of interest accrues on your Freshman 1 loan in the 54 months between origination and deferment. But importantly, interest accrues on *each* of your eight student loans. The table below shows the interest accrual for each of your eight $10,000 student loans during: (i) school and (ii) deferment.

Total Accrued Interest Of Student Loans

	During School		Deferment	
Semester	**Months**	**Interest ($)**	**Months**	**Interest ($)**
Freshman 1	48	3,231	6	471
Freshman 2	42	2,554	6	415
Sophomore 1	36	1,972	6	365
Sophomore 2	30	1,474	6	320
Junior 1	24	1,275	6	343
Junior 1	18	860	6	303
Senior 1	12	460	6	238
Senior 2	6	253	6	260
Total ($)		**12,079**		**2,714**

As shown in the table above, your eight $10,000 student loans will accrue interest totaling $14,793 ($12,079 while a student and $2,714 during deferment). Before further exploring interest accrual and capitalization, we must cover one additional, related interest topic: subsidization.

If your student loans are **subsidized**, the federal government will forgive all interest accrued while you are enrolled at least part-time in school. For example purposes, imagine all eight of your student loans are subsidized. Resultantly, your lender would forgive the $12,079 of interest accrued while you were a student, but not the $2,714 of interest accrued during deferment.

However, not all federal student loans (and no private student loans) are subsidized. While not a universal rule, most federal: (i) undergraduate student loans are subsidized, while most (ii) graduate student loans are unsubsidized.

With interest accrual and subsidization behind us, we can now revisit, and conclude: interest capitalization. Importantly, when you begin repaying your student loans, *any unsubsidized, accrued, unpaid* interest will be capitalized into additional outstanding principal.

For example, assuming your Freshman 1 loan is *unsubsidized*, and you begin making required monthly payments immediately upon graduation, the $3,231 of accrued interest would be added to your $10,000 of outstanding principal, resulting in $13,231 of outstanding principal.

Your Freshman 1 loan would thereafter amortize with a 7% APR on $13,231 of outstanding principal instead of your original principal of $10,000. Thankfully however, most undergraduate student loans are subsidized, so let's explore subsidized capitalization before returning to and completing our exploring of unsubsidized capitalization.

Presuming your Freshman 1 loan is *subsidized*, and assuming you begin repayment immediately upon graduation, your required monthly payment would be $116. Resulting in a total payment to your lender of $13,933 over ten years consisting of $10,000 of principal and $3,933 of interest.

However, if you waited until the end of deferment to begin making required monthly payments, $471 of accrued interest would also be capitalized, making your required monthly payment $122. Resulting in a total payment of $14,589 over ten years consisting of $10,471 of principal and $4,118 of interest.

Capitalizing your deferred interest from just your subsidized Freshman 1 loan might seem inconsequential, given over a 10-year term your Freshman 1 loan deferred interest results in you owing only $656 ($14,589 - $13,933) more to your lender. But let's explore the effect of capitalization if your Freshman 1 loan is *unsubsidized.*

If your Freshman 1 loan is unsubsidized, and you begin repayment immediately upon graduation, your required monthly payment would be $154. Resulting in a total repayment of $18,435 over ten years consisting of $13,231 of principal and $5,204 of interest.

Even if you begin repayment of your unsubsidized Freshman 1 loan immediately upon graduation, you will owe your lender an additional $4,502 ($18,435 - $13,933) more over a 10-year term than if your Freshman 1 loan was subsidized and you begin repayment immediately upon graduation.

Further, if your Freshman 1 loan is unsubsidized, and you wait until the end of deferment to begin repayment, your required monthly payment would be $159. Resulting in a total payment of $19,091 over ten years consisting of $13,702 of principal and $5,389 of interest.

Deferring repayment of your unsubsidized Freshman 1 loan until the end of deferment will result in you owing your lender an additional $5,158 ($19,091 - $13,933) more over a 10-year term than if your Freshman 1 loan was subsidized and you begin repayment immediately upon graduation.

Freshman 1 Loan Capitalization Scenarios

	Required Monthly Payment ($)	Principal ($)	Interest ($)	Total Repaid ($)
Subsidized				
Upon Graduation	116	10,000	3,933	**13,933**
Deferment	122	10,471	4,118	**14,589**
Unsubsidized				
Upon Graduation	154	13,231	5,204	**18,435**
Deferment	159	13,702	5,389	**19,091**

The table above merely summarizes the four repayment scenarios we just explored. Importantly, we have only been discussing capitalization of your Freshman 1 loan. Let's now spend some time exploring the effect capitalization and deferment has on each of your eight student loans.

Capitalization and deferment of each of your other seven subsequent $10,000 student loans will each result in hundreds to thousands of dollars of additional principal and interest over your 10-year term depending on: (i) if your student loans are un/subsidized and (ii) when you begin making required monthly payments.

For example, if your student loans are subsidized and you begin repayment immediately upon graduation, over a 10-year term you will pay your lender a total of $105,378 ($80,000 principal + $25,378 interest) with a required monthly payment of $878.

Alternatively, if your student loans are unsubsidized and you defer repayment for six months, over a 10-year term you will pay your lender a total of $124,864 ($94,793 principal + $30,071 interest) with a required monthly payment of $1,041.

Thus, if you defer unsubsidized loans your required monthly payment will be $163 ($1,041 - $878) more than if you immediately begin repaying subsidized loans. Further, you will pay your lender $19,486 ($124,864 - $105,378) more by deferring for six months than if you immediately begin repaying subsidized loans.

I know. I promised plain English. I know. Let's take a breather and step back from the flurry of numbers we just covered. Let's cover (in plain English) four key takeaways.

First, consider avoiding needing student loans at all by taking advantage of trade schools, community college, grants, and scholarships. Second, if you do use student loans to pay for college, try to obtain subsidized student loans to avoid capitalization of unsubsidized accrued interest.

Third, each semester you need a student loan results in a separate, additional student loan; each likely with a different APR. And finally, the longer you defer making required monthly payments for your student loans results in paying hundreds to thousands of dollars more in interest and principal over a 10-year term.

Also, keep in mind you will have multiple required monthly payments (one for each of your eight student loans). If you prefer to have one APR and one required monthly payment, consider **consolidating** all your student loans into a single student loan with a single APR. Just make sure your consolidated APR is lower than the weighted average APR of your multiple, original student loans.

Conclusion

Debt is a tool you can use to accelerate: (i) personal consumption or (ii) business growth. For this acceleration, you owe interest to your lender. The higher your APR, the more interest you will owe. And more interest means a higher required monthly payment.

However, just because you have enough income you *can* use to make required monthly payments for your debt, does not mean you can *afford* your debt. You cannot afford your debt if your required monthly payments are equal to most of, or exceed, your monthly income.

In fact, most lenders will not lend to you if the sum of your required monthly payments will exceed 35% to 50% of your monthly gross income. Further, borrowing for consumption combined with not saving and investing is a recipe for being broke. Though, as we saw in this chapter, successful business borrowing for growth is a recipe for richness and wealth.

Moreover, as we will cover in the next chapter, successfully using debt has advantages. For example, the more positive history you have with debt, the better your APRs and credit card rewards will be. However, there are consequences if you fail to make your required monthly payments in full and on time. Let's deepen our understanding of debt by exploring: creditworthiness.

Creditworthiness

Introduction

To complete our understanding of debt, we will now discuss creditworthiness. **Creditworthiness** is a borrower's ability to, and likelihood of, repaying debt. Hopefully you can appreciate there is always a chance a borrower (you) will not repay the amount borrowed.

For example, a borrower might lose their job (and thus their earned income), still want to repay their debt, but simply be unable to repay because they have no income. Alternatively, a borrower might have enough income to repay their debt, but simply refuse to repay their loan for any number of reasons.

Regardless *why* a borrower fails to repay their debt, a borrower **defaults** when they fail to make a required monthly payment in full and on time. For example, imagine you loaned me $100 but I stopped paying you back after I repaid only $60. When I stopped paying you, I would have defaulted, and you would have lost $40 of principal and the unpaid interest I owed you.

Every lender assumes the risk of default whenever they lend to a borrower. Lenders do two things to reduce their risk they will not be repaid: they (i) assess the creditworthiness of the borrower and (ii) structure the required monthly payment to include more interest earlier in the loan's term. We will discuss both, starting with: required monthly payments.

Required Monthly Payment

We have already briefly explored required monthly payments when discussing amortization. As a quick refresher, we learned the proportion of interest and principal repaid varies from month to month. We will now explore this variation in a little more detail.

Importantly, this variation is not arbitrary, and is instead a discrete mathematical calculation based on your loan's: (i) term; (ii) principal; and (iii) APR. Moreover, this variation is structured by design to prioritize payment of interest by the borrower. Let's explore further by revisiting our $300,000 home loan with a $1,432 required monthly payment.

Remember how in Month 1, your $1,432 payment consisted of $1,000 of interest and only $432 of principal? Well, it is not until Month 153 (nearly 14 years into our 30-year term) that your required monthly payment consists of more principal repayment ($717) than interest ($715).

For further comparison, consider the difference between principal and interest in your final monthly payment, which consists of just $5 of interest and $1,427 of principal repayment. Astonishingly, by Month 153 (only 42.5% through our 30-year term) you will have have paid your lender 61.7% of the total interest you owe ($133,046 of $215,609), while having only repaid 28.7% of principal ($86,088 of $300,000).

Without amortization, required monthly payments would consist of proportional percentages of total interest and principal owed. For example, over your 30-year term you will pay your lender interest totaling $215,609. Thus, combined with your $300,000 of principal, your total paid to your lender will be $515,609.

Resultantly, total interest paid accounts for 41.8% ($215,609 / $515,609) of your total paid, with total principal repaid accounting for the remaining 58.2% ($300,000 / $515,609). Proportionally then, your required monthly payment would consist of $599 ($1,32 * 41,8%) of interest and $833 ($1,432 * 58.2% of principal.

By Month 153, with or without amortization, you will have paid your lender a total of $219,096 ($1,432 * 153). However, without amortization, this $219,096 would have consisted of $91,582 ($219,096 * 41.8%) of interest and $127,513 ($219,096 * 58.2%) of principal.

Were you to default in Month 154, without amortization, your lender would have received only $91,582 of total interest compared to having received $133,046 of total interest with amortization. And remember, your lender will foreclose if you default and sell your mortgaged (collateralized) home.

So, should you default in Month 154, amortization results in your lender receiving $41,464 ($133,046 - $91,582) more interest than without amortization. Thus, your lender's risk of you not paying the total interest you owe is decreased using amortization. We will now discuss how lenders further reduce their risk they will not be repaid by: assessing creditworthiness.

Creditworthiness Assessment

In addition to amortization, lenders reduce their risk by assessing borrower's creditworthiness before agreeing to originate a loan. To assess a borrower's creditworthiness, lenders perform a credit check (in addition to perhaps other checks, for example, a background check). A **credit check** consists of your prospective lender reviewing your credit: (i) report and (ii) score.

A **credit report** is a detailed list of all your outstanding debts. For each of your debts, the details include the: (i) original loan principal; (ii) outstanding principal; (iii) required monthly payment; (iv) type of loan (for example, home versus student); and (v) payment history (have you made your required monthly payments in full and on time?).

Most lenders perform a credit check by contacting a credit rating agency. **Credit rating agencies** are businesses which: (i) collect the loan details in credit reports and (ii) calculate credit scores. **Credit scores** are a single number calculated using all of the information in a credit report.

To explain by analogy, your credit score is to your credit report what your final letter grade is to a semester of homework, quizzes, and a final exam. Lenders use your credit score as an initial assessment of your creditworthiness. With credit scores, higher is better. The higher your credit score, the more creditworthy you are presumed to be. The lower your credit score, the less creditworthy you are presumed to be.

In fact, it is quite common for lenders to wholly reject (delcine) a borrower with a credit score below a certain threshold, without ever reviewing the borrower's full credit report. Thus, it makes sense for us to discuss how credit scores are calculated, so you can achieve a high credit score.

As mentioned earlier, credit scores are calculated using the information in your credit report. Thus, it is crucial to remember everyone has a unique credit score based on their individual credit report. Specifically, credit scores are calculated based on the following five credit report aspects: (i) repayment; (ii) utilization; (iii) age; (iv) type; and (v) requests.

Repayment (often called payment history) assesses your payment of required monthly payments. Each required monthly payment paid in full and on time increases your credit score. While any late, unpaid, or less than full required monthly payments lower your credit score.

Utilization assesses your outstanding principal as a percent of your original loan principal (outstanding principal

/ loan principal * 100). To explain, let's revisit Month 153 of your $300,000 home loan. If you recall, in Month 153, you repaid $86,088 of total principal, meaning your outstanding principal is $213,912. Thus, as of Month 153, your home loan's utilization would be 71.3% ($213,912 / $300,000 * 100).

Importantly, each loan has its own utilization, though an aggregate utilization is also calculated. Credit scores and utilization are inversely correlated: the higher your utilization, the lower your credit score; the lower your utilization, the higher your credit score.

As I am confident you appreciate by now, your outstanding principal decreases each month by the amount of principal repaid with each required monthly payment. So, assuming you make all your required monthly repayments in full and on time, your credit score will increase as your utilization(s) decrease.

Age (often called history) assesses how new or old your credit accounts (debts) are. For example, if you applied for and were approved for a new credit card in just the last month, lenders cannot evaluate your creditworthiness based on this credit account because it is too young to have any history.

However, lenders will be able to assess this credit account after several months or years of you using your credit card and (hopefully) making all your required monthly payments in full and on time. The general idea here is, older credit accounts increase your credit score, while newer credit accounts decrease your score.

Let's step back for a moment and recenter. You should be able to see repayment, utilization, and age are somewhat intertwined: increasing your score the more you repay over a longer period of time, and decreasing your score when your debt is brand new and mostly unrepaid. Now let's explore the last two aspects of credit scores: type and requests.

Type assesses the subject matter of credit accounts on your credit report. Lenders consider certain types of debt positive, while other types of debt (comparatively) negative. For example, student loans and home loans are considered positive compared to consumer debt (for example, credit cards or personal loans).

Also, having a variety of different types of credit accounts is generally a positive factor for your credit score because it means a variety of lenders believed you were creditworthy enough to loan to. However, having too many outstanding debts can be negative, especially if these credit accounts are new (short history/age), have mostly unpaid balances (high utilization), or have missed, late, or underpaid required monthly payments (repayment/payment history).

Requests (often called inquiries) assess your requests to open new credit accounts. The general idea here is numerous, repeated requests for credit implies you have minimal savings or income. While minimal savings or income imply your ability to repay debt is low. And a low ability to repay debt reduces your creditworthiness.

Think of it this way: as a kid, when did you ask your parents for $20? When you already had $20? Or when you had $0 but wanted $20? If you already had $20, you probably would not have asked your parents for $20. And if you (the borrower) have to ask your parents (your lender) for $20, you probably intend to spend $20, and thus will not have $20 in the future to repay your parents.

Thankfully, your parents will not check your credit report or credit score to decide if they will give you $20. However, lenders do check your credit report and credit score when you apply for a loan. There are two important types of credit requests: (i) hard and (ii) soft.

A lender will perform a **soft inquiry** on your credit report and credit score when you ask for: (i) an estimated APR (ii) for a potential loan. Because you are merely *asking* for an estimated APR, and not *applying* for a specific loan, this soft inquiry does not count against you as a genuine request for credit.

However, should you decide to actually apply for a specific loan, your potential lender will perform a **hard inquiry** against your credit report and credit score so the lender can thoroughly evaluate your creditworthiness. However, your lender will not bother to perform a hard inquiry if their soft inquiry shows your credit score is below the minimum they require to originate a loan.

A Closer Look At Credit Scores

Like most topics we have explored in this book, credit scores themselves could easily be an entire chapter, if not an entire book. But as you should have come to expect by now, we will focus on covering only the fundamental credit score concepts everyone should know.

For starters, everyone has two primary credit scores (FICO and VantageScore) and many (upwards of 50) secondary credit scores. Secondary credit scores are used by lenders to assess your creditworthiness for specific types of credit. For example, one of your secondary credit scores is specifically for vehicular credit, which a car dealership might use when evaluating your creditworthiness for a car loan.

But more often than not, lenders just use one of your primary credit scores instead of any secondary credit score. And while there are two primary credit scores, in 2020, FICO is the most commonly used primary credit score.

FICO Credit Score Ranks And Ranges

Rank	Range	
Poor	300	579
Good	580	669
Great	670	739
Very Good	740	799
Excellent	800	850

As the table above shows, FICO scores range from 300 to 850 and are ranked from Poor to Excellent. Oookaaay. 300, 850, poor, excellent. Huh?! Why should you care? Why are credit scores important? Credit scores matter because credit scores determine: (i) the amount and type of debt you can borrow; (ii) the APR(s) you will be charged; and (iii) what, if any, fees and collateral lenders will require from you.

The higher your credit score, the more principal you will be approved to borrow. Further, you will be charged a lower APR with fewer, less expensive fees and collateral. The lower your credit score, the less principal you will be approved to borrow. Moreover, you will be charged a higher APR with more, more expensive fees and collateral.

Keeping Up With ~~The Gardashians~~ Your Credit

Remember those credit rating agency businesses which: (i) collect the information used for credit reports and (ii) calculate credit scores? Well, there are only a few major credit rating agencies, including: Equifax, Experian, and TransUnion. Unfortunately, despite their best efforts, sometimes these credit rating agencies are inaccurate.

For example, if a credit rating agency incorrectly includes someone else's debt(s) on your credit report, both your credit report and credit score will be inaccurate. Similarly, a credit rating agency might fail to include debt you owe, again resulting in an incorrect credit report and credit score.

Or even worse, someone could have stolen your identity and fraudulently borrowed money while pretending to be you, resulting in debt on your credit report that is, but is not, your debt! Resultantly, it is important to monitor your credit report and credit score regularly.

Thankfully, credit reporting agencies are required to provide you with a free credit report once every twelve months. Moreover, there are many free and low-cost services to help monitor, manage, and improve your credit report and credit score. I have included a list of resources and tools related to monitoring your credit report and credit score in the Appendices.

Conclusion

Do not always use credit, but when you do, use credit responsibly. Responsible use of credit is straightforward: make each required monthly payment in full and on time. Over time, month after month, your credit history will develop, your credit score will rise, and you will owe increasingly less outstanding principal.

Financial Planning

Introduction

Finances are like a toddler, both are incapable of managing themselves. Thankfully, unlike an unruly toddler, your finances will obey whatever rules establish. The purpose of a financial plan is to create a set of rules (and guidelines) for your finances, including how you will: (i) earn your income; (ii) spend your income; (iii) save and invest your income; and (iv) manage your investments.

Said another way, a **financial plan** documents the relationship you want to have with your finances. If life is like a road trip, then a financial plan is equivalent to your route. You can choose amongst multiple routes on your way to the final destination of your road trip.

Some routes are faster and more direct. Other routes take longer but are more scenic. And some routes are unplanned and full of both good and bad surprises. With road trips, there is not necessarily a right or wrong route.

The road trip route(s) you take depends on the type of experience you want. Similarly, your financial plan can be whatever you want it to be. You may choose to spend more and save and invest less. You may choose to earn more and spend more. Or you may choose to earn more and invest more.

The balance and plan you choose for your life is entirely your decision. With just a small amount of up-front effort and planning, you can create a financial plan that helps you maximize your ability to have whatever relationship you want with your finances.

Regardless the relationship you want, establishing a financial plan is fundamental to successfully managing your finances because, as the adage goes, "failing to plan is planning to fail." Because unlike surprise detours on road trips that merely waste your time (or perhaps result in a happy surprise), life's financial surprises are usually unplanned expenses.

Now do not get me wrong. Even with a financial plan, life can still throw you unexpected expense curveballs or a lost job or income. As the great poet Mike Tyson puts it, "everyone has a plan until they get punched in the face." But without a financial plan, life's financial gut punches will feel more like a knockout.

Financial Situations

While everyone's financial situation is unique, it is not. Everyone (you included) broadly fits (with some crossover of course) into one of three financial situations: (i) you are in debt; (ii) you live paycheck to paycheck; or (iii) you have income you save and invest.

You Are In Debt

If you are anything like me, you do not sleep well at night knowing you have required monthly payments lasting into what seems like eternity. Setting money aside in a savings account with a 1% APR is a losing proposition when you have debt with a 20% APR.

If you save money at 1% instead of paying off your 20% debt, you guarantee yourself a 19% loss! Lose 19% per year for a couple of years, and you will be one broke bloke.

On that note, paying off higher-interest debt before paying off lower-interest debt seems to make sense if you are in debt.

So how do you pay down debt? Well, you stop unnecessary spending. You already have multiple watches. You do not need another purse. You certainly can live without a $4 latte *every* day. And do not even bother trying to convince me *multiple* happy-hour drinks after work with friends is a necessity; you will survive with one or no drinks while still enjoying the company of your friends.

If you are in debt and you keep spending, how can anything but more debt result? If you want something bad enough, nothing else matters. If you are unwilling to reduce your spending and divert those now unspent dollars to pay down your debt, you simply do not want to be out of debt badly enough to ever actually achieve being out of debt.

Alternatively, instead of (or in addition to) reducing your spending, you may choose to increase your income. For example, you may choose to get a second job or work additional hours at your current job. Either (or both!) reducing your expenses or increasing your income will result in additional income you can use to pay down your debt.

Nobody said getting out of debt would be easy, or fun. Listen up. Getting out of debt will require sacrifice and pain. It will hurt. As I mentioned in the Preface of this book, I know first hand the pain of getting into, and liberation of getting out of, debt.

But debt pain is temporary *if* you repay your debt. And those who are tough enough to endure and overcome the pain of debt will experience the joy of financial freedom of being debt-free.

While I was paying off my vehicle debt, I was inspired to keep going by a quote hung in the hallway of my grandparent's house which read in part, "when the going gets tough, the tough get going." So what are you waiting for? Get tough, and get going!

You Are Living Paycheck To Paycheck

You are debt-free. Congratulations! But, your expenses match your income. You are living paycheck to paycheck. Not ideal. You have little, if any: savings, investments, or financial plan.

Even at this improved position compared to being in debt, it can still be challenging to see any light at the end of the tunnel. You are likely too busy working too many hours for your income to take time to consider a different way of life.

Let's illuminate a few paths forward. First, if you were in debt, and are now debt-free (congratulations!), starting to save is easy. For starters, simply save and invest the income you previously used to repay your debt. Simple!

Second, if you are *literally* living paycheck to paycheck, the basic advice for those who have debt similarly applies to you: reduce your spending and increase your income.

Finally, you do not need to eat out several times a week, you can live without every cable television channel, and you can certainly survive without multiple monthly subscription services. Which is to say, lifestyle moderation will magically provide income to save and invest.

When first beginning to save, the first financial plan most financial advisors will advocate you do is create an emergency fund. An **emergency fund** is a savings account with a cash balance equal to three months to one year of living expenses. These emergency funds are for when you lose your job, have a surprise medical bill, or otherwise incur a large, unexpected expense.

An emergency fund should be a new saver's priority. But to reiterate, paying off all debt is priority number one before starting to save. Because you are already in an emergency if you are paying 20% APR on debt you have yet to repay. So, pay off your debt first. Then build up an emergency fund.

You Have Income You Save And Invest

Congratulations! You have no debt, do not live paycheck to paycheck, spend less than you earn, and have income you save and invest. Most licensed financial advisors will tell you the first thing you should do is, nothing.

Just keep saving your income and evaluate what is important to you. For example, your top priorities may involve buying a home, going back to school, planning for retirement, or starting a new business.

As mentioned previously, at this stage of one's relationship with money, the approach is highly personalized to what each individual wants to achieve. After some thoughtful consideration of what your priorities are, memorialize your conclusions in a financial plan.

You Need A Financial Plan

Regardless your current or desired financial situation, you will benefit from having a financial plan. Do you earn income? Do you have expenses? Would you enjoy being richer and wealthier? If you answered "Yes" to any of these questions, you will benefit from having a financial plan.

It does not matter if you earn, spend, or want $100 or $1,000,000. You will benefit from having a financial plan! Having a financial plan is the first step to achieving a healthy relationship with your finances. And when you have a healthy relationship with finances, it becomes easier to fulfill your core values and accomplish your life goals.

More likely than not, you work 40 hours or more per week to earn the majority of your income. You owe it to yourself to create a financial plan precisely *because* you spend so much time earning your income.

Because without a financial plan, you will spend countless hours working, and your income will disappear into the great abyss called life (expenses). And after years of exchanging your time for income, you will have little to no savings and even fewer investments. And without substantial investments, you will always be stuck exchanging your time for income.

Comprehensive financial plans include substantial planning and documentation, financial advisors, and usually attorneys who help create, obtain, and manage: budgets, wills, trusts, prenuptial agreements, insurance policies, investments, powers of attorneys, advanced medical directives, and more. But for our purposes in this book, we will focus on one component of a comprehensive financial plan: budgets.

Budget

Most people have encountered the word "budget" before. But unfortunately, much like people's distaste for dieting, most people bemoan budgeting. But diets and budgets are simply *tools*.

A diet is but one tool (along with exercise) which helps people achieve a healthy body. Similarly, a budget helps people achieve a healthy understanding of their incomes and expenses. And remember, a budget is only one part of a comprehensive financial plan.

From the highest-level perspective possible, a budget contains two fundamental categories: (i) income and (ii) expenses (which includes saving and investing). Having made it to this point in this book, you should be familiar with: (i) income (currency you receive); (ii) how most people earn their income (exchanging their time); and (iii) how investors earn their income (investments).

From here, the next step to creating a budget requires you to: (i) identify and (ii) group (categorize) your expenses. You will encounter no shortage of approaches concerning budget categorization on the Internet if you spend even just a few minutes researching budgets and expenses.

Perhaps the most common categorization approach involves generic percentage allocations per expense category.

For example, these generic perspectives often look something like either of the tables below:

Example Categorical Expense Allocations

Category	**Percent (%)**
Shelter	40
Transportation	15
Food	15
Insurance	10
Lifestyle	10
Saving/Investing	10
Total (%)	**100**

Example Need/Want Expense Allocations

Category	**Percent (%)**
Needs	70
Wants	20
Saving/Investing	10
Total (%)	**100**

While general recommendations are likely a reasonable starting point, general recommendations certainly do not consider your personal needs and wants. Besides, regardless your initial percentage allocations, an investor continually attempts to increase the amount they save and invest. Which if you recall, increased income to save and invest will result from any combination of: (i) increasing your income and (ii) reducing your expenses.

How To Create A Budget

Creating a financial plan for the first time can be a daunting task for some. Many people get overwhelmed because they do not know where to start, or worse, people are scared to admit to themselves how much they are actually spending on certain categories.

While no two financial plans are precisely the same, it is essential to start somewhere. And I believe that starting point is a budget. Perhaps the easiest way to create a budget is not to create one at all. That is right! Moving forward, let's throw out whatever preconceived notion you have about what a budget is, how to create a budget, and what a budget imposes on you.

Instead, start by simply focusing on assigning a category to each of your regular, recurring expenses. For example, regular, recurring expenses include: rent, car payments, insurance, et cetera. While you are doing this initial categorization, *do not* fret about if you are spending too much, or earning or saving too little. In no time at all, and without even trying to create a budget, you will have created an initial budget!

You will be able to compare your categorized expenses against the generic percent allocations in the tables above. And you are now in a position to begin to decide if you should be earning more income, reducing your expenses, or saving and investing more.

For those interested in developing a budget using a spreadsheet, I created a budget template using Google Sheets (which you can download for Microsoft Excel). Additionally, many online services simplify the initial categorization step (along with many other helpful features) by enabling you to import your bank account and credit card transaction histories. For your convenience and consideration, I included in the Appendices a non-exhaustive list of several of these online budgeting services, along with a link to my budget template spreadsheet.

The Difference Between Needs And Wants

Needs are things we cannot survive without, for example: food, water, and a place to live. **Wants** are things we prefer to have, for example: fancy food, ice-cold water, and a mansion.

Everyone *needs* food to eat. You may *want* to eat at expensive restaurants, but you will live just fine buying groceries and eating at home. Everyone *needs* water. You may *want* fancy bottled water, but you will live just fine drinking tap water. Everyone *needs* a place to live. You may *want* to live in a mansion, but you will survive just fine in an apartment or small home.

Identifying and reducing wants is usually the part of refining a financial plan most people dread. Many people despise reducing the wants they buy because their financial relationship is a relationship of spending. Spenders experience happiness by spending their income on expenses.

And while investors may still choose to forego wants, investors enjoy buying needs because buying needs means investors can save and invest more. But unlike spenders who derive happiness by spending their income on expenses, investors derive happiness by spending their income on investments. And I thoroughly enjoy shopping for and buying my investments, just like spenders enjoy shopping for and buying their wants.

Perhaps the simplest way to have more income to save and invest is to stop buying wants and start buying needs. Wants almost always cost more than needs. So, without having to exchange any more of your time for income, you can increase the amount you save and invest simply by reducing your expenses. But remember, the wealthy focus on earning more income (especially passive, recurring income from investments).

For anyone who finds it challenging to reduce your spending, consider the following approach. Given most people earn their income by exchanging their time: think of expenses in terms of how much time you must exchange to make your purchase. For example, any time you want to buy something, ask yourself if purchasing X thing is worth working X hours to buy it.

For example, imagine you earn minimum wage, which we will assume (after income taxes) is $10 per hour. You could easily need to work *more* than an entire day (ten hours) to earn $100 to pay for just a single date night out, consisting of: drinks ($25), dinner ($50), and a movie ($25).

Alternatively, you can also have an enjoyable date night consisting of a romantic, candle-lit dinner at home, consisting of a: bottle of wine ($15), homemade pasta dish ($30), and online movie rental ($5).

Two great date nights: one costing $100 and the other $50. And despite being very different prices, both fulfill the need for a date night. However, the $50 date night results in both a date night and $50 to save and invest! But regardless how you choose to spend your income, paying yourself first *before* spending is an extremely effective habit to ensure you save and invest.

Pay Yourself First

Perhaps spending less and earning, saving, and investing more is easier said than done for many people. But permit me to share with you a habit which has made saving and investing effortless for me. This habit is to: pay myself first. Warren Buffett succinctly explained the **pay yourself first** habit when he encouraged, "do not save what is left after spending, spend what is left after saving."

Let's explore paying yourself first with an example by analogy. Imagine for a moment you are given a handful of ice cubes. In front of you, you see a: (i) freezer and (ii) glass of water sitting on a counter. What do you do with the ice cubes? Well, it depends on what you want. Do you want a glass of: (i) ice-cold water; (ii) somewhat cold water; or (iii) room temperature water?

If you want ice-cold water, you will place all the ice cubes into the glass of water. If you want somewhat cold water, you will place some of the ice cubes into the glass of water and some of the ice cubes into the freezer. And finally, if you want room temperature water, you will place all of the ice cubes into the freezer.

Over time, any ice cubes you place into the glass of water will melt and become water. While any ice cubes you place into the freezer will remain frozen as ice cubes. Real-life is very similar to the ice cubes and glass of water scenarios. Like placing all the ice cubes into the glass of water, you can spend all the income you make and not save or invest anything.

Alternatively, like placing some ice cubes in the glass of water and some ice cubes in the freezer, you can save and invest some of the income you earn and spend the income you do not save and invest. Unavoidably, in real life everyone needs to drink water, and everyone has expenses.

"Cool analogy bro, but just how is water and ice cubes related to paying myself first," you might be wondering? Well, if you earn some income (ice cubes) and place all your income (ice cubes) into the glass of water (expenses), when you come back later at the end of the month, all your ice cubes (income) will have melted into the water (expenses) which you drank throughout the month.

With no ice cubes or water, all you are left with at the end of the month is an empty glass and no ice cubes in the freezer (savings). Conversely, consider paying yourself first by putting some ice cubes in the freezer *before* placing any ice cubes into the glass of water. This way, no matter how much water you drink (expenses), you will always have ice cubes (savings and investments) chillin in the freezer.

But remember, water is a need and ice-cold water is a want. So, sure, you may *want* an ice-cold glass of water on a hot day, but you will still enjoy somewhat cold water, and all you *need* to survive is room temperature water. This water temperature truism of need versus want applies equally to finances (which we have already discussed). Remember that mansion, exotic sports car, and designer purse?

Just remember to continually appreciate saving and investing is not a: sacrifice, chore, burden, or dreaded task. Saving and investing is a privilege *everyone* can take advantage of. Remember, just about everyone can save and invest $1,378 or more per year. And it is your responsibility to decide how much of a priority in your life you will make saving and investing.

Conclusion

Now I am not telling you that you need to *completely* quit spending your income on new watches, purses, or $4 lattes. But how about a less expensive watch? One less purse? And $4 lattes only on the weekend as a reward for making $1 coffees at home on the weekdays?

Many people have a negative, or unhealthy, relationship with money. People often have excuses about why they cannot succeed financially and refuse to take responsibility for, and exercise control over, their financial situation. Do any of the following sound familiar?

"I do not make enough money"
"I spend all my money"
"I cannot save enough money"
"I will not be able to retire"
"The stock market is too risky"

People regularly receive financial advice, yet dismiss the advice as impossible or inapplicable. Paying down debt, saving for an emergency fund, and investing 10% to 30% of your income can seem impossible when you are living in debt or paycheck to paycheck.

Similarly, even if you have money to invest, the multitude of investment options can be overwhelming. Inexperience can paralyze people from achieving financial progress and perpetuate unhealthy relationships with money.

Imagine this: you earn enough income to pay all your bills ahead of time, with plenty of extra income for fun, saving, investing, charity, and whatever else you desire. When bills arrive, you pay them without batting an eye.

Further, you have cash savings equal to six months of living expenses and fully fund retirement investment accounts. You have the freedom to make choices in your life not based on price tags, but based on passions. This type of life is absolutely possible for you no matter your current financial situation.

If you doubt this possibility for even one second, go reread Laozi's truism at the beginning of You And Money. If you doubt financial success is possible, financial success will be more impossible for you. If you believe financial success is possible, you will put forth the effort required to make financial success a reality for you.

For the religious, think of it this way: if you pray to the Almighty for patience, do you think the Almighty will give you patience, or opportunities to be patient? Now this is not to say that if you simply *believe* you will be wealthy, wealth will just start falling like manna from the sky. The law of attraction has no chance of working without both intense focus *and* action.

But, the first step toward achieving wealth *is* believing you can develop and maintain a healthy relationship with money. You have likely heard the saying, "money does not grow on trees." The true meaning of this saying is: money cannot be obtained out of thin air. But sticking with the money tree analogy, money *can* be grown like a tree.

Ask any arborist how to grow and care for a tree, and the abridged version of the explanation you will receive is, "plant a seed, water and fertilize a maturing sapling, and finally, prune your full-grown adult tree." Translating the arborist explanation into money terms would look something like this: start saving whatever small amount you can, grow your savings, start investing, and finally, manage your investments.

The problem for most people is, most people do not have the mental fortitude to grow their money tree. You see, we live in an instant society. Instant communication: text messages. Instant entertainment: Netflix. Instant knowledge: Google. Same-day delivery: Amazon. Expeditious customer service: the DMV.

We hear on the news about the latest lottery winner: instant millionaire. We see the rich and famous gallivant around on television and social media: instant popularity. People want to have lots of money, now, today, yesterday! But a tree does not grow in one day, rather, day by day.

Similarly, building wealth is a gradual, daily process that does not happen instantly. Building wealth requires patience, planning, and purposefulness. Building wealth does not happen by accident. Building wealth is a choice and lifestyle. You have to choose to develop, and live out, a healthy relationship with money if you want to be wealthy.

Whatever your situation may be, letting go of old excuses and beliefs that perpetuate poor financial habits, and adopting a new, positive money mentality, is the first step in achieving your financial goals. The changes you will need to make depend on your specific, current financial situation.

With utmost sincerity, I truly hope this book empowers you to make more informed financial decisions and achieve wealth beyond even your loftiest expectations.

While ruminating about your ideal financial plan, consider American businessman John Rockefeller's perspective, "[(s)he] who works all day, has no time to make money."

Conclusion

Putting It All Together

I have never been one for saying, "goodbye." I usually part ways with, "until next time." And until next time in a book I suppose, would be to encourage readers to visit: https://www.fundamental.finance/

However, I read somewhere on Reddit that authors should avoid upselling their other amazing products at the end of their book. But seeing as how I do not do goodbyes, and I am not supposed to conclude with an until next time by upselling https://www.fundamental.finance/ (which I would never do), I was at a loss for how to conclude Fundamental Finance until my best friend came to the rescue.

Coming to my rescue, my best friend convinced me I should part ways with some personal commentary to really connect with you. So, because my best friend is never wrong, I will leave you with brief, personal comments regarding each chapter of this book.

Saving And Investing

There are three truths: (i) the rich earn more; (ii) the wealthy invest more; and (iii) you, yes, *you*, can be both rich and wealthy if you accept responsibility for your financial future and choose to save and invest.

The best time to start saving and investing is when you start earning income. The second best time was yesterday. Next best, today. Not tomorrow. Not next week. Not next month. Not next year. *Today*.

Time Value Of Money

Compounding is undeniable. The secret to success is picking something and working on it for years. Excellence is a compound effect. The repetition and refinement of simple, ordinary behavior yields extraordinary results.

The sooner you save and invest, the sooner you will be rich and wealthy. But good luck being rich or wealthy if you do not invest. But in addition to compounding your finances, remember to compound (and manifest!) your knowledge. Just remember to have fun along the way.

What Money Is

Learn more. Share more. Create more. Do more. Earn more. Live more. *Knowledge* is money, and *currency* is used to value, store, and exchange knowledge. Pursue money, not currency. Currency is attracted to money.

In an alternate universe, I will have never manifested the accumulated knowledge required to write this book. Let alone even accumulated this knowledge in the first place. But thankfully, in this universe I did. And you and I are both better off for it. If you want to earn it, you have to learn it.

You And Money

You can work for your money. Or your money can work for you. Your choice. Just remember if you choose to put your money work for you, investing is a habitual lifestyle. And if, even after reading this book, you do not want to commit to saving and investing, that is cool. No hard feelings. Enjoy scrolling Facebook and binge watching Netflix.

No less than 30% of all income I earn is immediately saved and invested. And every investment return I generate is reinvested so it can compound. I do not spend what I want, only to save and invest what is left over. Instead, I save and invest what I want first, and spend what is left over.

Earned Income Taxation

Pay your taxes. Failing to pay your taxes can result in financial penalties and prison time.

Unearned Income Taxation

Tax-advantaged investment accounts are awesome; use them. Each year, to maximize tax-advantages, my savings get deposited into the following accounts order by priority: (i) HSA; (ii) 401(k), up to my employer's matching contribution; (iii) IRA(s); and all remaining savings end up in my (iv) brokerage account.

Debt And Credit

Debt is a tool. The rich and wealthy use business debt to increase their income. Everyone else uses debt to buy things they do not need to impress people they do not like.

Creditworthiness

I have had the same credit card my entire life, never carried a balance, and wear the same pair of shoes every day. You do the math.

Financial Planning

Life is difficult (DOTA 2 is way easier). But you can make life easier for yourself by paying yourself first (and giving yourself a raise whenever possible). Knowing how much you can pay yourself is impossible without a budget and financial plan. I make a budget and financial plan each year.

Appendices

Supplemental Resources

These are the supplemental resources I highly encourage you to explore in addition to, or if you absolutely insist, in lieu of, Fundamental Finance. These supplements are listed alphabetically based on their title along with their latest-available hyperlink as of December 2020:

Everything You Need to Know About Finance and Investing in Under an Hour
https://www.youtube.com/watch?v=WEDIj9JBTC8

Finance and Capital Markets
https://www.khanacademy.org/economics-finance-domain/core-finance

How The Economic Machine Works
http://www.economicprinciples.org/

Introduction to Investing
https://www.investor.gov/introduction-investing

Investing 101: A Tutorial For Beginner Investors
http://www.investopedia.com/university/beginner/

Saving and Investing

https://www.sec.gov/investor/pubs/sec-guide-to-savings-and-investing.pdf

Budget Resources

I am not recommending you use any particular service(s) or even a service at all. The following list is ordered alphabetically and is provided only for your convenience and consideration:

Budget Template Spreadsheet

https://docs.google.com/spreadsheets/d/1X3xMkNfkzuBy3naiiL15I9b_vLKrX-4f_IFR1JucWqo/

Dollarbird

http://www.dollarbird.co/

Be sure to check out Dollarbird's calendar-based user interface.

Goodbudget

https://goodbudget.com/

Be sure to check out Goodbudget's educational content.

Mint

https://www.mint.com/

Be sure to check out Mint if you use TurboTax.

Mvelopes

http://www.mvelopes.com/

Be sure to check out Mvelopes's monthly-coaching plan.

Pennies

http://www.getpennies.com/

Be sure to check out Pennies's minimal user interface.

Personal Capital
https://www.personalcapital.com/
Be sure to check out Personal Capital's investing software too.

PocketSmith
https://www.pocketsmith.com/
Be sure to check out PocketSmith if you love to explore "what-if" scenarios.

Simple
https://www.simple.com/
Be sure to check out Simple's online banking too.

Tiller
https://www.tillerhq.com/
Be sure to check out Tiller if you want to use Google Sheets.

Wally
http://wally.me/
Be sure to check out Wally's collaboration features.

You Need A Budget
https://www.youneedabudget.com/
Be sure to check out You Need A Budget's educational content.

Debt Resources

Miscellaneous
https://studentaid.gov/

Lenders
https://www.commonbond.co/
https://www.avant.com/
https://www.earnest.com/
https://www.laurelroad.com/

https://www.lendkey.com/
https://www.marcus.com/
https://www.prosper.com/
https://www.sofi.com/
https://www.upgrade.com/
https://www.upstart.com/

Creditworthiness Resources

Credit Score

https://www.creditkarma.com/
https://www.creditsesame.com/myfreecreditscore/
https://www.myfico.com/
https://www.self.inc/

Credit Report

https://www.annualcreditreport.com/

Douglas Denhartog, Esq

Since 2010, I have invested thousands of personal, professional, and academic hours and energy learning and using the financial concepts explored in this book. The hundreds of hours I spent writing this book focused on curating, organizing, and simplifying the most important financial concepts everyone should know.

After completing my undergraduate in 2011, I spent four years wrangling financial data as a business analyst until enrolling in law school in 2015. In 2018, I completed law school with emphases in business and tax law. Since completing law school, I have been a tax consultant at a multinational professional services firm and obtained a license to practice law from the California State Bar.

https://www.denhartog.com/

https://www.fundamental.finance/

Made in the USA
Monee, IL
04 November 2026

67386600R00098